rue story of a rare

patient
ben watt

the true story of a rare illness

Grove Press
New York

First published in Great Britain by Viking in 1996
First published in the United States by Grove Press in 1997

Printed in the United States of America

Library of Congress Cataloging-in-Publication Data
Watt, Ben, 1962–
    Patient : the true story of a rare illness / Ben Watt.
        p.   cm.
    Originally published London : Viking Press, 1996.
    ISBN 0-8021-1612-4
        1. Watt, Ben, 1962–   —Health.   2. Churg-Strauss syndrome—Patients—
Great Britain—Biography.   I. Title.
RC694.5.I53W38   1997
362.1'9613—dc21
[B]   96-46771

Grove Press
841 Broadway
New York, NY 10003

10 9 8 7 6 5 4 3 2 1

R0125745472
mw

For Tracey

Special thanks to Tracey, my parents Tom and Romany, Jennie, Charles Mackworth-Young, Rod Hughes, Chris Wastell, Nick Law, David Lindsay, Silé (Sheila) Taylor and the National Health Service. Additional thanks during the book's completion to John Collee, David Godwin, Tony Lacey, David Eldridge and Alexandra Pringle.

PREFACE

Everyone is shocked by their first real hospital experience. When I was seven I fell off a wardrobe trying to find an Action Man and I remember a green-stick fracture in my arm, the trip up to Queen Mary's, Roehampton, and the excitement of proper plaster of Paris to take to school the next day. And I remember the three hours waiting with a severely twisted knee after a football match as a teenager, the same injury a few years later when I needed physio, and the occasional winter chest X-ray. But none of these instances can count as a real hospital experience: I didn't really make it on to the mountain. I saw Accident & Emergency (or Casualty as it is often called) and witnessed put-upon nurses, senior house officers and doctors called in from elsewhere with their ties loosened and top buttons undone, daytime drunks, kids with their mums, sweating relatives, people with nothing wrong with them, people with something seriously wrong with them but they didn't know it yet. I didn't even get a proper bed – I didn't need one – just a chair or maybe a hard trolley. (I always wondered why they had to be so hard until I found out it's to help them get their hands under you to flip you over in theatre, should you get that far. They are not meant to be beds. They are meant to be worktops.) And the trolley would have had a strip of green absorbent paper for a sheet,

ix

pulled off a wide roll, and I probably stared at the back of a piece of curtain material half-pulled across my cubicle and caught sight of someone doing exactly the same across the corridor. And mostly I got away within a few hours, out on to the cool street again, not really very unwell, real people walking by, buses, super-sensing the journey home, maybe bandaged with any luck – to at least show I'd been in the wars.

I was in a bad car crash when I was eight. That took me a little way up the mountain. The crash happened in Scotland, on the way to the swimming-baths in a suburb of Glasgow. I was on holiday. My mum and dad were in London. My grandfather was driving. My grandmother was in the back seat. I was in the front, my feet up on the dashboard. We were in a Mini. We approached the lights at the crossroads, the lights went red, and my grandpa just seemed to accelerate. I heard my grandma shout, 'Will!'

When I came round, there was a crowd around the car. A tiny trickle of blood was on my ear. Hundreds of small crystals of glass like transparent cane sugar were all over my lap. The car wasn't in the middle of the junction but pushed well over, as though we'd turned left but sideways. There was a double-decker bus stopped too. My grandpa wasn't speaking. The bus had hit his side of the car on the junction, side on. The steering-wheel was very near me, touching against my leg. It seemed odd to have the steering-wheel that close to me, like it had been positioned in the middle of the car for use by either passenger. My grandma was lying on her side on the back seat. She was saying something to me. Her shoulder seemed tucked behind her back. An egg yolk was dripping off the seat, and there were peas on the floor. My legs were scrunched up on the dashboard. I always travelled with my feet up. They had stopped me being thrown out of the car.

I couldn't tell how much time had passed. It felt like a minute, but it must have been a while for the ambulance to have already got there. A woman I'd never seen before helped me out with an ambulance man. I was barely marked. She'd been a passenger on the bus. We had to wait while they cut my grandpa out. In the ambulance he opened his eyes for a second and said everything would be all right, but then he closed them again. He was very pale. The liver spots on his balding head stood out. His fine, wispy white hair was messed up like he had been sleeping on it. He didn't have his glasses on any more, which made him look less like him.

I didn't see him again after that. The woman who helped me out of the car stayed with me at the hospital until Great-auntie Peggy arrived from across town in Knightswood. Grandma and grandpa had been taken away. A nurse put a sticking-plaster on my ear and they X-rayed my skull. I talked to some men in the day-room and fingered the bump on my head. I thought it was odd that they were in dressing-gowns and pyjamas in the middle of day, all men together watching TV. Watching TV in the middle of the day with my pyjamas on was something I only dreamt of. One of them bet me a bottle of Scotch that Chelsea wouldn't beat Real Madrid that night. I didn't know what Scotch was.

Back at Peggy's, later on, I was allowed to stay up and watch the match. The European Cup-Winners Cup Final 1971.

Chelsea were my team. Ossie, Charlie Cooke, 'The Cat', Chopper Harris. I'd been looking forward to it, but Peggy only had a black-and-white set with a funny fish-eye picture. I didn't enjoy it much, but I was allowed to eat sausages in front of it. My dad arrived. He had flown up. I heard him talking to Peggy in the kitchen. I remember him being furious – not with her, but with my grandpa for endangering my life, his son. I didn't often hear him raise his voice.

The next day he sent me home on a plane on my own. I was looked after by an air-hostess. She gave me a BEA key-ring. My grandma had dislocated her shoulder. My grandpa died in the hospital on Intensive Care.

Even bearing in mind the impression that it made on me as a young boy, I still regard this story as a mild hospital experience, only one foot on the mountain. Much in the same way I look on my wisdom-teeth operation in my mid-twenties, when I went in for the day but as an out-patient only. All four wisdom teeth were to come out in one go. I had my first general anaesthetic – I felt like a big shot – and found myself recovering on a day-ward with two other people my age, with a mouth and tongue like shoe leather and a head like towelling. By the end it had been an adventure. I had even put a jacket and tie on to go down to the hospital and had treated it like a special day out. I was charming to the nurses because I knew I would be home by teatime, and I was too – overpampered when I got in, flowers from Tracey, an unnecessary bed made up and ready should I have felt poorly, which of course I didn't. The teeth had almost fallen out. 'Like honeycomb,' the surgeon had said. I was out at the pub by eight o'clock.

It is the first time they keep you in that really matters. Overnight is when you are really on the mountain. It makes you lose your bearings a little more. It is the unfamiliarity and the institutionalized accessories that first get to you – starched pillowcases with the hospital's name on, theatre gowns, walls of fake-gaiety get-well cards, tablets served in a tiny plastic cup like the top off a bottle of Night Nurse, the smell of heavily washed floors and sterilization. It seems so primitive, so unlike home, so barely adequate. And how those reassuring words from the doctors who send you in ('Oh, you'll be in and out in twenty-four hours. You won't notice you've been in') seem so misleading as you lie trying to sleep for the first time in a room with only half the lights turned off at night and nurses whispering. And the little things we're in for turn out to be not so little after all. An endoscopy. A laparoscopy. A miscarriage. Keyhole surgery. 'It's nothing,' they say. But they all bring invasion. Scraping around and needles; disorientation and sutures. We can't wait to get home.

ONE

It's June 1992. I am lying perfectly still on top of the sheets on a wide, clean bed in a private hospital near Harley Street. I have my shirt off. I am having a heart test – an electrocardiogram. The nurse has just left and sent a doctor to see me. The doctor has just popped her head round the door and asked me if there is any history of heart disease in my family. I said no. She tells me she won't be a moment. The door closes. I am twenty-nine. A few minutes pass. A man enters. He is wearing a crisp pink shirt with a white collar. He has kind eyes and a racing-driver's moustache. He looks like he knows a thing or two. He smiles and sits on the edge of my bed. There is bad news and bad news. The bad news is he thinks I am in the middle of a long, slow heart-attack, and the bad news is, if not, then he thinks I am about to have a massive one. I smile back.

I have had difficulty walking and breathing for ten days. Pains in my chest. Pains in my belly. Aching pains in the joints in my left arm. In my calves. I've been clutching hot-water bottles, sitting under a blanket staring out at the garden. I've been rocking back and forth on the kitchen chair for sometimes three-quarters of an hour, pressing my hands against my ribs, crying, talking to myself out loud, telling Tracey not to worry. She has stood before me, pale, not knowing whether to act. Later, I have lain in bed with the light out, Tracey beside me, and stared up at the dark ceiling, and listened to her staring too.

My lungs feel raw. I am taking massive doses of inhaled steroids.

I

My asthma has been chronic. The other day I cried in front of my GP and walked out. I am seeing an acupuncturist twice a week. Yesterday I cried in front of her. She says my energy is alarmingly low. Last week I saw a homeopath. I told her all I know. I began at the beginning. She gave me tablets. Since then my asthma has improved but the pains have increased. Is this meant to happen? Is it even connected? I don't know what to do. The taxi was late. I had to rush. I had no breath. I walked like an old man. In the waiting-room, I had to ask the nurse for a glass of water. I read the property pages in an out-of-date Country Life, *and now I have been told I am having a heart attack.*

In many ways that appointment at the London Clinic was really the end of a beginning that had been going wrong since Christmas. I'd been a mild asthmatic for a few years, but as the new year came I was unable to climb the stairs and my lungs were just aching all the time. I would often wake in the night gasping for air, inhaling as though through thick gauze, and for a week in January I had to stay in bed all day, weak and still, frightened to breathe. I was treated with three strong anti-biotics for a possible chest infection. They did nothing. Probably viral, my GP said. All the same, I moved from the basic Ventolin inhaler to the harder stuff – Intal, Serevent then Pulmicort. When my GP finally referred me to a consultant chest specialist, after four more bad weeks and two short courses of oral steroids, my symptoms were confirmed as still nothing more than those of a recognized asthmatic with a history of hay fever – I'd had skin-prick tests in 1989 following bad sinus problems, which had detected a not-uncommon hypersensitivity to household dust mites. The chest specialist gave me turbohalers. The big ones. The 400s. My GP didn't want to pay for them.

Things improved temporarily. I took a week's holiday in Crete, thinking warm fresh air would help, and even flew to Japan with Tracey and the band to play ten days of concerts where I couldn't take deep enough breaths to sing all the words. But within another fortnight I was home again and in trouble. I went back and asked the chest specialist how serious he thought things were. He said four out of ten. I couldn't believe him. I was up to 3;200 mg of inhaled steroids a day.

At home we tried to keep the house scrupulously clean, vacuuming and dusting three times a week. We bought a special vacuum cleaner for asthmatics, as well as bedding and pillows that discouraged house dust mites. I bought my own peak-flow meter to monitor the strength and puff in my lungs and just watched my breath get shorter. I would flake out early in the evenings, my body gripped by lassitude and viral pains in my shoulders and my elbows. All day I would monitor my food intake, trying to find a pattern that might link my asthma with something I was eating. I avoided dairy produce, caffeine, red wine, shellfish, oranges and tomatoes. I tried supplements – multivitamins, evening primrose oil, garlic oil.

By May, all evening meals were leaving me wheezing badly. My eyes would be shot with blood for twenty or thirty minutes at a time. I would have fast furious sneezing attacks – repeated sneezes one after the other, bang, bang, bang, for four or five minutes. I took up the Alexander Technique to try to relax and to open my lungs a bit more. I had a few lessons and would finish supper by lying on the floor with my knees up, trying

3

to calm the pounding in my chest, the palpitations in my arms and my flushed neck and face. Friends would come round and I'd say it was normal.

In the days running up to my electrocardiogram my asthma suddenly seemed to ease off. It was like a storm passing over. I thought maybe the homeopath's tablets were working, but on the afternoon before the test I had forty minutes of chest pain like never before. I called the chest specialist myself and told his secretary I had to see him. I thought it was an emergency. I'd pay privately. She fitted me in that evening. I went down with Tracey. The taxi-driver thought we must have just argued we were so quiet. We were both scared. The consultant was measured and calm. My distress seemed to make no impression on him, but he arranged a private chest X-ray and an ECG for first thing in the morning. That night at home I lay curled up in the middle of the bed and thought if I took one more breath my chest would burst open.

Even so, looking back on that morning at the London Clinic I couldn't help thinking I was being wheeled fully clothed to a waiting ambulance for the wrong reasons. A heart attack seemed so removed from my experience and, moreover, the homeopath had said I'd get worse before I got better. I was a young man, a treatable asthmatic, not an old man with a weak heart. A bed had been found for me in the Coronary Care Unit at Westminster Hospital. The unit at my local hospital, the Royal Free, was full, with three waiting. *Coronary Care? How old was I? It must be a mistake.* Cruising through central London I felt bewildered. The ambulance man asked if I felt OK. I said I supposed so. It was summer outside. Tracey was on her way.

When we arrived it was midday. The place was humming with people. I was checked in by a receptionist and left against the wall by the men's loo.

'You be all right?' said the ambulance man as he was going.

'Yes. What now?'

'Don't try and get up. Sit quiet and someone will be down in a minute. Take it easy.'

He left.

Take it easy. Don't try and get up. I sat calmly in the wheel-chair, expecting a seizure at any moment. He'd left me facing the wall. I felt humiliated. Disabled. A pool of water was seeping from under the loo door.

A nurse came for me. Up on the heart unit I was told to get undressed 'slowly' and to lie down 'gently'. Curtains were pulled round the bed. It was close and hot. I listened to voices, and watched the feet below the curtain as they hustled back and forth. A male nurse in a white tunic arrived with a trolley and another ECG machine. He took out a yellow Bic razor and began shaving little tufts off my chest with no water or soap. I was fitted up with half a dozen suckers, each wired into a multicore leading to the machine. I thought of little toy bows and arrows. Some of the suction pads wouldn't stick, so a bit more hair was shaved off. I could feel my heart beating. I kept thinking I could hear it stopping.

Tracey arrived. She had my soft grey shorts in a carrier bag. We sat behind the curtain. She had chased me across town, arriving at the London Clinic expecting a calm chat with a doctor only to be told I'd just been taken to Westminster Hospital in an ambulance.

My pulse was taken and a thermometer was slipped in my mouth. My blood pressure was read through a huge black Velcro tourniquet. The male nurse left. He asked if I wanted anything. I said not really, but then stopped him as he was going and said a wire coat-hanger for my clothes. He looked surprised but said he'd fetch one. I thought everyone was talking about me – such a young man on a coronary care unit.

Two doctors arrived. One sat on my bed, the other stood. They looked like they'd been brought in from pressing work. They each wore blue pyjamas and a shower-cap. The one standing had on white plastic clogs. *Are these people doctors? Is this what they wear?* The doctor sitting in front of me had a hot, damp face. He looked straight at me. He seemed kind. His eyes were intensely concentrated in the moments he was talking. He asked for pain descriptions, a little history.

After they left, a young nurse came with a clipboard and a Biro. She had a little questionnaire for me. She wrote slowly in fat, rounded, teenage handwriting, touching the corner of her mouth with the tip of her tongue as the pen hit the paper. 'My name and background'. 'My date of birth'. 'My self-image'. 'Was I afraid of dying?'

By the evening the initial moment of crisis seemed to have passed. I was now on the NHS. It was a Friday. I irrationally wanted to go home. Hospital had frightened me. It had all got too serious. I wanted control back, but I agreed to stay on the Coronary Care Unit (CCU) for observation over the week-

6

end. The doctor in the pink shirt at the London Clinic, Dr Sutton, was also the unit's consultant heart specialist, and I was being looked after by his team. I sat up in bed in grey marl shorts. I wouldn't lie down. I tried to look fit. I was sure nothing was wrong with my heart and that the sooner I could convince them and get away the better. I remembered how the homeopath had talked of the body exorcizing illness, bringing poison to the surface before it can recover. I thought if I could put this hoax scare behind me I could sort out my asthma on my own again.

On the third day Tracey arrived in the morning with Eileen, our manager at the time. Wimbledon was on the silent TV up in the corner of the room. I had slept very badly and was starting to get bad indigestion, belching, acid stomach and severe backache. I thought a walk would do me good. More tests had already seemed to prove that the cardiac signals had been a false alarm, and, although I was giving very strange blood results, the pleuritic pains in my chest had calmed down again. Doctors were now guessing at gallstones or a gastric ulcer – something less critical. The nurses were understandably reluctant to let the three of us go out. I was still a patient on CCU after all. I smiled as winningly as I could and argued I might well be discharged on Monday. It was a quiet Sunday. They said OK.

We took it easy down the corridors and into the lift. Down in the garden, though, I suddenly felt strangely weak. It was an unusual fatigue that swept over me, from somewhere deep and central. It was like a bucket from a well coming up dry, as though my body was finally saying, 'No more now. It's time to stop pretending.' I had to sit on a bench. I wanted to sag forwards. Pigeons waddled across the path. A leaf fell. After a few minutes, Tracey and Eileen took my arm and we all walked slowly back to the unit in silence.

That night the pains in my back moved to the front. A young surgeon was sent to see me. It was late. He was tired. He flipped me over and kneaded my belly. I'd been constipated for two or three days. He said he could feel crap in my bowel. I slept badly again. I couldn't lie on my front.

The next morning the unit was like a beehive. Dr Sutton's houseman was just back from holiday. He had a lot of catching up to do. Rushed off his feet, he took blood from my arm ham-fistedly. I snapped at him. I was taken up to another floor for an endoscopy, to check for ulcers. A fibre-optic snake was passed down into my stomach under sedation. Back on the unit I was garrulous and loud under the effects of the drug –

'Ha ha ha. I woke up in the middle. I woke up in the bloody middle. Are we back already? Which is my bed? Here? OK. Not this one? Don't let that bloody bastard back with the needles. Fat git. Who's in charge? You? Well, don't let that fat git take any more blood. I woke up in the middle, you know. Lie back? Why? I am lying back. I felt the tube scraping around in my stomach. It's a bit warm, isn't it? Is it hot in here, or is it just me? Can I go home? Can I go home today? There's nothing wrong with me. They've got it all wrong. Don't tell me to be quiet. Just keep that fat one with the needles away from me. He doesn't know anything. Ha ha ha.'

The endoscopy found nothing irregular, but my blood counts were still coming back with big abnormalities. Marked

8

signals were being given out that my body was under some kind of attack. A group of my white cells, the eosinophils, were showing up in numbers far greater than one would associate with the allergy responses of a regular asthmatic. Moreover, as my asthma seemed to have mysteriously subsided over the past week, the doctors were particularly puzzled and quizzed me some more. I told them I had recently been to Japan, where on a previous trip I had suffered severe food poisoning. This would tally with my results. A sleeping parasite reawakened or worm infestation could also cause such hypereosinophilic activity. It was decided I should be moved on to a general ward for tests and observations. A parasite specialist from Immunology would see me.

They moved me on to Marie Céleste Ward. I was sitting on a temporary bed in the corner against the wall in the packed room. It was in the middle of the meal round during the same evening. The air reeked of meat and boiled potatoes. The TV was on loud. We all had to raise our voices. The doctors were uncertain as to their next move. This upset me. They decided to move me into the side-room – partly out of compassion, partly for fear of contagion – and to run some more tests. They left. Tracey ate my dinner.

The hospital was due for closure within a matter of months and the building was in decline. My side-room was shabby. The blind lay broken on the floor; dry Sellotape was stuck to the frames where someone had tried to fix it back up. There was a yellow sealed bucket for used needles under the sink, a paper bag for a bin. The windows were coated with the film of car exhausts. That night I barely slept. I watched the staff in

9

the offices across the road finish work, shut down computers, turn off lights, and then later watched the lights all come on again in the same offices as the night cleaning staff arrived. The fluorescence would flicker across my room.

When my mum first came to see me the next day, she turned to the window and sighed dramatically, 'How depressing.' I realized that nobody who came to see me in those first few days really knew what to say. I remember Toby, my half-brother, his wife, Yvonne, and the children standing at my bedside – little Luke unhappy and disorientated in Toby's arms. I can't remember them saying anything, nor me.

Rumours had inevitably started spreading already – heart attack, mystery virus, stress. Simon, my eldest half-brother, rang. He never rang. He lived in Scotland. I knew that my mum must have told him. I took the ward phone. He jumped straight in –

'Ben, what are you playing at? Isn't it time you packed it in?'

'What? What do you mean?'

'You know. The pop thing. All that lifestyle nonsense.'

'Simon, what are you talking about? What do you mean "lifestyle nonsense"?'

'Oh, come off it. You're only twenty-nine. You're killing yourself. You must be crazy.'

'What?' I was speechless. 'You think I've had a heart attack, don't you? Who told you this? I haven't had a heart attack. They know that much at least.'

'Yes, but it's all related. The music business. You should take it easy. You're still young.'

'But it's got nothing to do with the music. I'm not overworked. I'm fine. Well, not fine but . . . '

'What is it then?'

'They don't know yet. I've got strange blood readings.'

'Well, you should take it easy anyway.'

His wild guesses were incensing me. The noise in the corridor was distracting. I found myself pressing the receiver harder and harder against my ear. I wanted him there, in front of me, to explain properly, but he was in Edinburgh and somebody wanted to use the phone. I was angry. The music business. Pop lifestyle. Who did he think I was? Some flamboyant flake gasping after fame and money, who had driven his car into a flotation tank and then had a seizure on the way to the bank? I suddenly found myself hating his adopted snobbery. I hung up. He once told mum how he thought 'the South' was just full of phoneys, and he was getting out.

Ultrasound and blood tests came and went, all of them blank or inconclusive. No ulcer. No gallstones. The results of the parasite tests were going to take a while to come back, but I still treated each morning like the one on which I would be discharged. I would get up ignoring new cramps in my gut and, instead of taking breakfast off the morning trolley, I would shuffle along to the ward kitchen when no one was looking to help myself to cold milk straight from the fridge, hot toast, cereal. I'd take them back to my room and set them up on the table by the sooty window and imagine that eating out of bed with a breakfast fetched by myself was a sign of my good health and individuality and that I wasn't dependent on the hospital yet. I thought it would stimulate my bowels and after a good shit everything would be all right and I could go home. But fatigue would overtake me and I'd lose my appetite and I'd have to climb back into bed.

At first I couldn't understand why doctors weren't called every time I was in pain. The staff nurses were kind and the student nurses young and keen to help, but both were untrained in diagnosis and when I'd call one of them with my call button they could offer no answers and I would get fractious and upset. Nobody told me that, except in times of emergency, the doctors only came round twice a day – once in the morning, once in the evening – and that only they could take big decisions. I had to learn the pace of the days.

One morning I got up and took a shower by padding across to the women's ward across the hall, and then called Tracey saying the doctors knew nothing and I was going to discharge myself and come home. Right there and then. She was calm – just told me to wait till she got there. By the time she arrived I was back in bed, bad again.

I imagined the nurses I passed in the corridor saying, 'There's nothing wrong with him. He should be at home.' One night, when I couldn't sleep and I was free of pain, I even crept back along to CCU and sat up with a couple of nurses, chatting and laughing in hushed voices, telling tales about my family, enjoying an audience, trying to be attractive. They were drinking tea. The only light was cast by an Anglepoise on the desk. I felt as though I'd slipped into a girls' dormitory after lights-out.

★

Over the next couple of days the abdominal pains started to become acute. I would have to kneel on a pillow by the bedside, my stomach pressed against the side of the mattress for comfort, my hands against my forehead, my body rocking back and forth. Sheila, the ward sister, would come in and stroke my head, make me drink Gaviscon, and stay until the pains had gone. The pain would come in bursts – sometimes slowly building, sometimes swift, but always lasting twenty minutes or so. I could feel my blood pressure drop, my face cool, greyness.

Sheila's presence reassured me. Sheila by the bed. Sheila kneeling next to me. Sheila in the doorway. Over those first couple of weeks her talismanic properties took on immense significance. She was tall. She wore blue. She was just a ward sister who lived in a flat with a tortoise and a husband who ran a pet-shop, but when she was on duty Tracey would call for her in my moments of intense pain or despair. I believed she really cared more than the other nurses. I believed she would make things better. It was never anything she said. It was something in her face. I thought she knew hospital secrets. When I heard the handle turn on the door to my room and she came to help me up off the floor and back into bed, or to hold my hand, to give me drugs, to stroke my brow, I wanted to be a child, to be safe, to be loved, to hide in the folds of her clothes. I wanted to have Tracey reassured, to have her told heaven and earth were being moved. Outside my room, in the flatly lit corridor or in the nurses room, I know she took my mum and Tracey aside and gave good news as even-handedly as she gave bad, and then consoled and listened. I felt she was keeping our heads above water, pulling us to the bank, her hand cupped under our chins.

David Lindsay, the senior registrar from CCU, took me up to Echo-sound to finally discount any cardiac problems. For the first time I asked for a wheelchair. I couldn't face the walk. The woman on the echo-sound machine gave me a representational image of my own heart. They saw nothing unusual. When I came down again I gave the picture to Tracey. David said the machine was very popular with doctors in the week running up to Valentine's Day. I thought the picture would be something I'd want to see again, but I don't like to think of it now. The blurred, grainy image makes me think of uncertainty and doubt, of the body as an unfathomable, mysterious place and the repository of too much that we don't know. It is like images from unmanned submarines that photograph deep ocean trenches, or from satellites that capture the dark craters and dust plains of outer planets, unknown and worrying, only it has my name printed on it.

My dad finally came to see me on his own. Mum had put him on the train, and he'd taken a taxi from Paddington. Like everyone else, he didn't really know what to say. He would clear his throat and plant his hands on his knees as if in readiness to speak, and then just sigh and grip my arm instead. The hospital freaked him. He followed us down to X-ray and sat forlornly on a bench next to Tracey while I went in. A gaunt man in a black towelling dressing-gown was coughing violently in the corridor. My dad has a weak chest. I could see him getting restless and unhappy. It was busy, and there were a lot of people about. When I came out, Tracey said my dad had left.

I got back to my room and was told there was still no diagnosis and they wanted a piece of my bone marrow. They gave me the same drug for the bone-marrow extraction as I had had for the endoscopy. A man just came the next morning and stood by my bed with a steel trolley and a big needle. One of the nurses held my hand.

'I'm not asleep yet. I'm not asleep. I can feel it. I can feel what you're doing. Don't start. Don't start yet. Please wait. Is it a big needle? Just wait a minute. What are you doing now? I am relaxed. Lie still? But I'm not asleep yet. Don't do anything. Why are you smiling at me? What's funny? Who's there? Is Sheila there? No, please don't even do a trial run. Hold my breath? Breathe in and hold, two, three, four. I can feel it. I hate it. I hate it. I can't help it. Yes, I am comfortable. Stop. Don't let him start. Wait. Please wait a minute. What do you mean it's all over? D'you mean you've finished? You have? But I'm not asleep yet.'

All the tests were drawing blanks. My eosinophils meanwhile seemed to be infiltrating multiple organs, and in astronomically high numbers. Eosinophils are not thought to be dangerous in their own right. They are white cells that appear in times of intense immune-system activity, usually where allergy or parasitic infestation is involved, supervising and relaying messages to other white cells from the body's defences. They are an easily detectable marker of invasion in regular blood tests, but as my asthma had disappeared and initial parasite tests showed nothing conclusive nobody knew if the eosinophils were a freakish but benign presence or signalling or even contributing to a still hidden disease or infection somewhere else in my body. It was like a phoney war. I suggested the homeopath's tablets might be working. They said they thought it unlikely, or at best coincidental. They were sure the remission of my asthma was part of a wider problem. If not, why the eosinophils? The term 'multi-system disorder' was used for the first time. I knew what was coming next. The HIV counsellor would come by later. I didn't want counselling.

The counsellor was a woman. Blue jersey crew-neck; striped shirt with collar up. She was articulate and gentle –

'This is all in the strictest confidence. Nobody will know your name. When the test is done down in the labs you will be a number, that's all. Can I just ask you if you have ever had an African girlfriend?' She knew what I did for a living and I imagine she envisaged a lifestyle. Unconventional. Generic rock 'n' roll. Occupational hazard.

'No. Never.'

'OK. Now normally the result would have come back within twenty-four hours – obviously you want to know one way or the other – but as it's Friday it's going to be Monday. Sorry. Will you be all right over the weekend?'

I wasn't scared. I just felt constipated.

Over the weekend I worsened, with hourly crippling cramps, heartburn and sweats. Sheila gave me an enema. The little tube was slipped up my arse while I lay on my side on a waterproof sheet. She fired off the liquid and I lay there for a few moments, unimpressed. Then my guts started tingling. Low down. I rolled off the bed and sat on the commode. A few hard stools and pellets shot out into the pan in a jet of water. It felt inconclusive. My abdomen then went into spasm. I doubled up and fell forwards on to the floor. Sheila helped me back into bed. It felt like someone was pulling drawstrings tight around my guts.

On Monday the HIV result came back negative. Somebody suggested eosinophilic gastro-enteritis, and the tests started to get worse. Under another sedative a long biopsy needle was inserted into my liver while I gibbered and whimpered away clutching on to a nurse's hand. I thought things like this happened in other rooms, under bright light with doctors in gowns, not in your own bed with the bedside lamp angled down on to the site for illumination by a man with his sleeves rolled up.

Blood was now being taken twice a day. Some of it was examined in the hospital; some of it was being sent to Scotland. While I was sedated for the liver biopsy the houseman had taken my blood and had tried to be clever, leaving a butterfly needle in my arm so he could use it again that afternoon and save me having to endure a fresh one. When I came to, my forearm had puffed up and there was nobody around. I screamed at the nurses and the needle was taken out.

I was taken for a CT scan, to take cross-sectional pictures of my gut. Following several trips to Ultrasound my regular porter had become a shy, bespectacled German called Gert. He was polite, quick in his movements, and told me he was over here trying to better his English. I saw him reading a book that seemed to be called *British Etiquette*. Did he push trolleys and wheelchairs with a full knowledge of cutlery placements and appropriate headgear for Royal Ascot? We sped along the

X-ray corridors. To prepare for the scan, I'd been made to drink radioactive orange juice and told to lie down for half an hour. Gert left me in a waiting-area.

I lay down on my side on a hard, low bed and pulled the baby-blue cotton blanket under my chin. It had a silky seam along the top. I thought of being a child again, curled up in the boxroom that later became my mum's study at our old house in Woodlands Road, and days off school with tummy-ache, waiting for her to call the school and tell them I wouldn't be in. A mother was in the room with her child. I wanted them to stop talking. The pain was bad.

A doctor came for me. I had to walk the last bit to the scan. I could hardly put one foot in front of the other. The doctor got impatient. They laid me down inside a big white doughnut and took X-rays as I moved through a fraction of an inch at a time. It took half an hour. Lying flat on my back was virtually impossible. I would nod off for a minute or two as my body shut down against the pain and would then come round again, disorientated and lonely. They kept coming out from the booth to push my knees down.

I was wheeled back to my room and vomited the radioactive orange juice all over the basin. Two young student nurses just stood looking at me pitifully from the doorway, like kids. Kneeling there by the basin, I felt I was adapting already, like a creature moving from sea to land, evolving a new identity. And I was sealing myself away. My sense of time and space was shrinking. The invisible thread that had been tying me to home and the desperate desire to get out had slackened. I became interested only in making things bearable for the next twenty minutes or so. I looked for moments of stillness, a subtle shift in posture that would bring minutes without discomfort. I looked forward to simple, basic things – dry, clean sheets; the feeling of leaning back on freshly plumped-up pillows; the moment of unwrinkling my brow. I found myself thinking of kidnap victims and enforced confinement, but felt no resentment or bitterness. I stopped doubting the seriousness of it all. I only wanted to understand, to focus my attention, and to learn the doctors' language and to be of help.

That Friday two doctors from the London School of Hygiene and Tropical Medicine came down. They confidently assured me that, in spite of no conclusive proof, I was bound to have a parasitic infestation. Although one parasite had already been discounted, further tests in Glasgow would confirm it, they said. I lay on the bed talking to a room full of people. I felt silly talking while lying down, felt I ought to sit up at least, but my belly was tight with fluttering cramps. I felt sure they were wrong, but how could I say it? The doctor who talked the most had a full beard and a 'Save Africa' badge on his lapel. They were all eager to take me over to their hospital, which had no facilities for an emergency. I really thought they didn't have a clue.

That night I went into a nosedive. The pains had turned into superhuman garrottes. I developed bad diarrhoea and would reel out of my room and into the ward loo, where the stench of shit and the trapped summer heat made me gag. The twelve hours that followed are hard to recall now, except that I remember asking the night staff to refill my hot-water bottle. The hospital wouldn't provide hot-water bottles, and so my mum had left my room around 9 p.m. in search of one and ended up in a taxi stopping at all-night chemists until she got to the Edgware Road. She got back with the only one she could find – a child's one, with a furry rabbit for a cover, called Bedtime Bunny.

I had started hiccuping. I couldn't stop. It went on into the next day and evening. I was so exhausted and sick from it I had one of the nurses call a night doctor. He was young, by chance his father had been a doctor who had written a paper on hiccups and he suggested I might try a drug used on mental patients to close the flap leading from the digestive tract to the stomach. I was so desperate I took it. It sent me to sleep for a couple of hours, but when I woke up I struggled to sit up and began hiccuping again.

Over the weekend I was virtually delirious with pain and diarrhoea. My pulse was fast and sickening in its intensity. I was hiccuping all day and night for hours on end. I remember nothing clearly. I see myself coming and going, Tracey beside me, no time, no real time, just flat agony and snatched sleep. Tracey says I was being given painkillers that were designed to obliterate. I don't remember taking them. I can see Sheila standing in the doorway from time to time.

The surgeons arrived on Monday evening. The doctors still hadn't come up with a concrete diagnosis; it was time to simply cut me open and see what was going on. When the surgical team arrived I couldn't even lie flat for an examination. I just cried and cried, huddled on a chair by the basin. A diagnostic laparoscopy to be performed by Prof. Wastell was planned for the next day. Tracey asked if they could do it straightaway. They said it could wait until morning.

TWO

Who is that? It is Tracey. Where am I? I don't know this room. I am warm. I am drunk. Who is that at the end of the bed? It is my mum. Why is she here? These pillows are soft. They must be the softest pillows. I am probably in America. Am I an angel? No, I am a bird. I am circling above. I am in a tree house at the top of the tallest tree in the widest forest. Everything is below me. There is my bedcover. The bed is like the countryside — fields and cars and little people. I am looking through a camera obscura, like at the beginning of A Matter of Life and Death. *Why is Tracey so small? An image at the end of a telescope held up against my eye the wrong way. I cannot speak. I must make my eyes wide and full of questions.*

I had lines running into the main artery in my neck, and a little clothes-peg on my finger that checked my pulse. A ventilator tube was plumbed into my mouth and throat. My upper body was wired up with electrocardiogram suction pads. I had a catheter in my cock, and lines and cannulae in my wrists for saline. Sunk deep into my chest was a food pipe. The last moment I remembered was an image of someone bringing me an operation consent form late at night. It seemed like weeks ago. I couldn't speak. All I can remember is drifting. Tracey spoke.

'Your bowel was bad,' she said.

I am circling above. I am part of a painting. Tracey and Mum are in the painting too. We are characters fanning out from the bed.

'You've had a lot of surgery, but you are getting better.'

I must be in America. We must be on tour. I am abroad. I must have collapsed abroad. No, I must be in the hospital for Tropical Medicine with the man with the beard and the 'Save Africa' badge, who said I had worms. I'm drifting again. Nobody loves me, everybody hates me, they think I've got worms . . .

'You are on Intensive Care.'

I am on Intensive Care? Intensive Care. I told them so. How glamorous. But I feel no pain. Something has been done. I am special and understood now.

Tracey had been given a little board with all the letters of the alphabet on it. 'You must tell us what you want. You must point to the letters,' she said.

I spelled out 'E-n-g-l-a-n-d?'

Tracey nodded and said yes.

I felt suddenly intensely lonely. I spelled 'S-a-d', and Tracey started crying a little bit. Then I spelled 'S-h-e-i-l-a?'

'Sheila's coming,' she said.

We were all quiet for a moment. Like a painting. My mum started speaking.

What is that my mum is saying? I cannot hear her properly. There is music playing somewhere. My ear hurts.

I spelled out 'I w-a-n-t t-o h-e-a-r . . . '

Tracey jumped in before I could finish. 'You want to hear us *talk* more? OK, we'll talk some more.'

I shook my head. It was a tiny movement. I tried again. My finger traced the letters. 'I w-a-n-t t-o h-e-a-r m-o-r-e . . . '

Tracey wouldn't let me finish again. 'You want to hear more . . .' (Her eyes flashed round the room.) '. . . more *music*,' she said. 'He wants to hear more music. Turn the music up, someone.'

No, no, no . . .

I shook my head again. I spelled out slowly. 'I w–a–n–t t–o h–e–a–r m–o–r–e t–h–r–o–u–g–h m–y l–e–f–t e–a–r.' My ear was folded into the pillow, muffling the conversation. Fogged up with drugs, I seemed unable to send a message to my neck to move my head enough to free it.

Tracey and my mum roared with laughter. I could hear relief and the release of tension. Tracey laughed again and rolled my head sideways a little way before resting it back on the pillow. I could hear the music more clearly now. It was Bonnie Raitt. Why was it playing? I knew that song. It was making me cry. I was spinning away again, thousands of feet above. Tracey took my hand. We were both crying.

Sheila came. She knelt by the bed and took my hand with her head on one side. Her eyes were full. She said nothing.

Even if your relative seems not to react to you, it is likely that they will be able to hear, and will be aware of their environment. It may seem strange to talk to someone who is not able to answer you, but this can help to comfort your relative, as can holding their hand. You will find lots of equipment. This enables staff to monitor the person closely, to give drugs and fluid and to help with breathing. The nurse will explain the equipment to you. There will be one nurse who will be with your relative at all times. Never feel that you are in the way. (ITU Relatives Leaflet)

★

Heavily sedated, I had been asleep for four whole days. Prof. Wastell had cut me open as planned, but had seen something so bad at first he'd simply stapled me back together again and sent me up to ITU (Intensive Care) to pause for thought. My small bowel had virtually rotted away inside me, and probably had been doing so for several days. The whole area, crippled by blood-vessel damage, had been severely infected with gangrene and peritonitis, poisoning my blood and threatening fatal perforation. Inflammation and the instability of the dead and matted tissue had made immediate access and repair almost impossible. Instead Dr Mackworth-Young, a consultant rheumatologist, and his immunology team had been called in straightaway to try to calm the area down with drugs overnight, to enable surgery to continue the following day.

It seems my immune system had been flipping out in some kind of massive overreaction. The eosinophilic warning signals had been right. Huge numbers of white-cell antibodies from my immune system's defences had been stimulated into attack by something unknown – an invading allergen or parasite possibly – but instead of their being regulated and then flushed out as usual, my bloodstream had been teeming with the harmful wrestling complexes they were forming, and they had settled in the tiny vessels and connective tissue surrounding my small intestine. As they'd raged on, blood vessels had become chronically irritated and inflamed and then consequently destroyed – a process known as vasculitis – and three-quarters of the small intestine (innocently caught up in the battle) had simply died from interrupted blood supply. It was as if a massive tourniquet had been tied around it.

24

My immune system, now aggressively triggered, had seemed unable to shut itself down and, more alarmingly, had begun to produce additional antibodies that had started to no longer recognize my own tissue. They had been destroying it, as if it too were the invading enemy. I had in effect become autoimmune. I was attacking myself.

Immediately following the exploratory operation, Dr Mackworth-Young had prescribed intravenous steroids to try to reduce the inflammation, antibiotics to fight the infection and a serious drug called cyclophosphamide that blocks cell growth in an attempt to temporarily stamp out my frenzied white-cell and antibody production and effectively knock out my immune-system activity. Hard-wired into a life-support system, my chances of surviving that first night on ITU had been put at 25 per cent.

The next day I'd been given a day's rest. I'd been showing signs of stress. Another operation straightaway had been deemed too risky. Although I'd been technically stable, if critical, the biggest threat at that stage had been a spontaneous unstoppable perforation of the weakened bowel wall that would have fatally flooded my bloodstream with septic fluid created by the rotting tissue.

The following morning I'd been taken straight up to theatre for a long operation. The Prof had removed large sections of the dead bowel and sewn the ends together as the drugs worked to stabilize the infection and damp down the rampaging immune system. Back on ITU, however, I'd shown no signs of improvement. My pulse and temperature had stayed high, signalling a continued struggle with the infected tissue.

Tracey had stayed day and night. So had my mum. Killing time. Waiting. Reading. Watching the monitors above my bed. Walking slowly by the river. Shopping pointlessly. Tracey says at night my face was like puffy candle wax, bloated by drugs and creased by the ventilator straps.

It had been clear that more was going to have to be removed. The following day the surgical team had gone in again and in another laborious operation had taken out another three or four feet of the necrotic bowel. At last I began to show signs of relief. Even as I was being wheeled back to the unit, Sheila, who had collected me, says she registered my fever and pulse falling in the corridor. The surgeons had, however, reluctantly now removed more than ten feet of my small bowel. What this would mean for my future, no one would predict.

The drugs had played their part too. Infection and inflammation had been contained, and the rioting immune system had at least been temporarily quelled. And so, with the remaining bowel stabilized and a cease-fire holding, the anaesthetists had reduced my sedatives and I'd opened my eyes on a Saturday afternoon on to a room I'd never seen before with no memory of any of this.

The afternoon they brought me round, after Tracey and my mum had sat with me with the letter-board for a while, I had an epidural – a spinal injection – fixed into my lower back to effectively paralyse me from the waist down and reduce pain following so much abdominal surgery. The grogginess had lifted. Before the epidural was put in, the nurses had been asking how I was feeling, did I feel pain, and at first I had felt nothing; but later I started to notice heat. My abdomen felt hot, and then hot and sore and pounding, and within an hour I started to feel shocked and frightened. I had a morphine pump. Grasping it in the hand like a computer-game joystick, I could give myself metered doses of painkillers. I pressed it all the time, but the system would only allow one pulse every ten or fifteen minutes. I remember I constantly expected to raise the bedclothes and see blood, with the dressing soaked through. My mind filled with images of gunshot wounds and blast victims and cauterized landscapes of still-smoking bomb craters. The anaesthetist came with the epidural. Nurses rolled me on to my side. I wanted to die. Tracey was there. The mattress was too spongy. The anaesthetist couldn't find the right spot. I felt his fingers pushing against my vertebrae. A nurse's hand was firmly on my shoulder.

I cried out, 'Is it done? Is it done yet?' I didn't know what was being done. I didn't know anything, flinching from the gentlest touch. I wanted to be in open summer fields, a sky above me, Tracey running in front, out of real time.

'Lie still. Lie still,' the anaesthetist was saying.

The mattress cover was like waterproofed tent material against my face. I was staring into the corner of the room. Later I remember rolling back and expecting to feel something sharp or something snapping off, but instead just lying there waiting for my legs to go numb.

Tracey left around nine. I couldn't sleep. I just stared and stared at the clock on the wall. I felt unique. I felt bored. Drugs were searing round my body. I felt as if I could throw back the sheets and walk out of there. I asked Mike, one of the nurses, to give me something to help me sleep. He said he wasn't allowed to. An hour later he came back. I felt like Gulliver under all the drips and feeds. I didn't dare move. I thought if I moved my stomach would split open. I said I had to sleep. He had a tiny needle on a grey cardboard tray in his hand. He leant over and emptied its contents into the arterial line running into my neck, saying, 'This should help.' I was about to speak again, and then seemed to look up to find three hours had passed.

They took me back to theatre to remove the last of the patches of bad bowel on the Monday morning. I was distressed and scared like a child who can't get on a plane. They put me under quickly, even before I left the unit.

I am five. I am asleep, half-asleep, in my room, a big room at the top of the house but divided in two by a stud-wall partition with glass windows along the top. The wall takes drawing-pins very well. I have two film posters from my mum on my wall – one with Clint Eastwood and Lee Van Cleef as cowboys. Lee Van Cleef is a strange name. My half-sister sleeps on the other side of the wall, but she is away. I am half-asleep but I can sense light flickering, butterfly light. I can smell burning – a burning like the paper twizzled tapers my grandma makes for the wood fire when we go away sometimes in the summer holidays. I can hear a pit-a-pat, a crackling pit-a-pat. It must be raining on the flat roof above. I cannot wake up fully. I dream on. The light still flickers. Yellowy flickering light. The smell is stronger. The rain must be really coming down now. I think I can hear it crackling in the huge copper beech in the garden outside.

I open my eyes. I don't understand. The wall at the end of my bed is on fire. My poster for The Good, the Bad and the Ugly *is full of flames. Faces are burning. The dry paper curls and spits. Smoke rolls up the wall and then strangely down again, like the plume of an exhaled cigarette. I sit upright, as if awakened by an electric charge. I can see the door. There are no flames near it. Only my wall seems to be on fire. I stare at the smoke. It now seems to run in a channel where the wall meets the ceiling, like the trail from the stack of a travelling steam train. It comes towards me, unfurling and rolling like a wave. I feel myself close my mouth. I am gripped for what seems like an age. The rolling tube of smoke. The blast of flame and paper at the foot of my bed. My room is filled with shadows and light. I jump out from the sheets and I am rushing from the room with my hands covering my head and down the stairs and I crash my fists against my parents' bedroom door. 'Fire! Fire!' I am shouting.*

My dad unlocks the door.

'Fire! Come now!'

He races up the stairs ahead of me and pulls a blanket off the bed and whacks the wall like a carpet-beater until the flames have gone and the room just smells hot and acrid. He picks up my child's night-light candle. The wax is all gone from it. The dish has burnt dry and melted the desktop. The corner of the desktop is all bubbly, like boiling treacle. Scorch marks streak the wall immediately above it, and higher up, where The Good, the Bad and the Ugly *once were, only a blackened patch is left. Flecks of ash and paper are on my bed. I look out of the window and see a dark, dry, still night and the big outline of the silent tree.*

Coming round from the anaesthetic some hours later I thought I could see two nurses moving around above me. There was a lot of activity. The reconnecting of lines and tubes, the smacking of latex gloves. It was bright. I heard voices. I was back on ITU, but it felt like somewhere else – like I was just below the water-line in a swimming-pool, unable to fully break the surface, figures above me distorted, faces rippling. The light was dazzling. White light like flaring magnesium. I had the tube from the respirator deep in my throat. It was unbearable. I felt like I was gagging continuously. I felt miles away from everyone, in a tunnel on the edge of waking. I thought I was several feet down into the mattress, and I wanted to reach out to attract attention like a drowner. I was trying to speak, trying to get them to understand that I must have the tube removed, but all one of them was saying was, 'Calm down. Lie still.'

I thought I was going to crap myself. Tracey came in. I grabbed at the alphabet board in her hand and spelled out 'S-h-i-t'.

'You feel shit? Yes, I'm sure,' she said.

No, no, no. I shook my head violently and pointed down the bed.

'You *want* to shit?' she said.

I nodded vigorously.

She asked for a bedpan.

It was slipped under my arse, but of course nothing happened. It was just a response to the anaesthetic wearing off. I pointed to the tube in my mouth.

Take it out. Take it out.

Tracey tried to soothe me. 'You have to show them that you can breathe on your own before they'll take it out.'

I was seething with indignation. I started breathing as fast as I could. In out. In out. I could hear the air in the ventilator like a snorkel. I had to regain control. I felt I was the victim of an overreaction. I needed no help. The nurses watched me for a while longer and then sat me up a little way. The elastic strap was loosened and then one of them eased the respirator free, my mouth wide, the length of plastic tubing knocking against my teeth as it came out. My throat felt sandpapered. I wanted to retch. I gulped in air and blinked in the bright light, Tracey holding my hand.

Angela, one of the nurses, took me outside the following day. She just came on duty and asked if I fancied a spin in a wheelchair. It seemed ridiculous. How could it possibly be allowed, a day after a week of major surgery? But I was so bored and strung out on painkillers, and my arse ached and my feet were all jumpy. It took fifteen minutes to get me disconnected from all my drips. Temporary stops and bungs were found. I was like a bathroom being capped off by a plumber. Sitting me upright, swivelling my legs round out of bed and into the chair took another five minutes. By the time I was ready I really wanted to get back into bed, but it was too late.

Tracey came too. We went out of the door. I took the spinal injection with me on my lap – a big syringe mounted into a carry-case, battery-operated, the fluid released from the chamber on a slow timer, running from the needle down a narrow tube into my back. I held it like a grenade. I could hear myself talking me through it –

But I've only just had my last operation. Does the Prof know? These corridors smell of cooked fat. I can smell oranges. Aren't the floors hard? There are ridges everywhere. I can't believe they've left the epidural in. I'd better not drop this box-pump. Is it feeding me painkiller now? Don't shut the lift doors on me. That's better. Hello, I'm on ITU. What? Outside? But I thought we would stay inside. Oh, OK then. Up and over the step. That's it. It's so loud. All these people on their lunch-hour. Life as normal. I don't like this. These paving-stones. I'm hunching. I feel like spun glass. Thin, transparent, breakable. Don't drop me, because I am powerless. I abdicate all responsibility for myself. You could tip me out and I'd just lie there. This is too far now. Can we go back? You can't get the chair over that step anyway. Turn around. Home now.

I began to get used to the language and routines. 'ITU' was short for 'Intensive Therapy Unit' and an alternative term for what I'd always called Intensive Care. I learnt that I had two bowels – a small bowel, sometimes called the small intestine, where all the digesting is done, and a large bowel, or colon, where the waste is processed. I'd always thought 'bowel' was just a colloquial term like 'guts' and meant somewhere near your arse.

The mornings would begin with the 6.30 drug round and the arrival of the nurses on the morning shift. Intravenous drugs were fed into my body through the lines and drips in my neck, chest or arms. Sometimes the fluids would feel as cool as stream water as they flowed up my arm; other times they would sting shockingly as they irritated my thin veins. The lines in my neck and chest penetrated so deep that I felt nothing at all when they were used.

I was often bad-tempered in the early mornings from no proper sleep. Nurses would try to wash me in the bed and I'd sulk. They'd brush my teeth for me and try to put a comb through my hair. I'd dribble the toothpaste into a cardboard bowl. I didn't see the point. Sometimes they'd wheel the TV over and turn on breakfast TV and I'd watch something profoundly irrelevant like the business news. It wouldn't even be light outside.

Gifts and presents that you may want to bring: Most people are unable to eat or drink normally. Please ask your nurse before bringing in food and drink. Flowers and plants are not a good idea because they can grow bugs in the water which can spread infection to the patients. Silk or dried flowers are a good alternative. Personal items of toiletries are a good idea, i.e. talc, perfume, aftershave, shaving foam, razors, toothpaste, etc. Bars of soap are not a good idea as they get soggy and may also grow bugs. Liquid soap in a dispenser is a good idea. Music tapes or tapes from the family, photographs and cards are good because they help the person to keep in touch with home. (ITU Relatives Leaflet)

I wanted nothing to get in the way of my long silent hours of search and re-evaluation. I was like an enormous tasking computer, sifting through its millions of data deposit boxes, temporarily inaccessible, freeze-screened, finding, replacing, paginating memories, the hospital monitors above my head flashing like the tasking icon, a busy bee, a spinning clock. I was unable to wear anything, my arms and neck and chest strung with drugs and fluids like a limp marionette, my cock stretched by a catheter, my thighs punctured by the needles

33

from anti-blood-clotting injections, my belly zipped up like a body-bag. I wanted no pretence at comforts. When the periods of momentary anger and searing boredom passed, I wanted to be humble. I wanted none of the trappings relatives are encouraged to bring, and days later, when I did gradually allow rewards back in, it was piece by piece – my ring, my soft slippers. Abstinence. Contemplation. Deprivation. They all seemed more appropriate.

There is not much space for the storage of personal property. While your relative is ill, they are unlikely to require many items. Hearing aids, glasses and a wristwatch or small clock are good things to have. It's often nice for the nursing staff to have a photo of the patient before they were ill to relate to. (ITU Relatives Leaflet)

The days of sedation and surgery bothered me, and bother me still. Where did I go for four days? To theatre and back, no doubt, but how can my mind offer no clue as to how I felt, up there so often, knocked out, and then back down to rest and sleep for days on end? I have no recurrent bad dreams, or nightmares of the surgeon's work. I endure no persistent, latent anguish or undue suffering. It is as though one day I closed my eyes and then on another I opened them again. No time passed, and the gap between the days is now neatly joined like edited film.

So does the body remember? Such invasion, such destruction and trauma – the cutting, the sewing, the bleeding – surely these must leave an imprint? Many alternative therapies and holistic approaches to medicine work from the basis of the body's memories. It is suggested that the body never forgets an awkward birth or a badly broken bone. Tension and stress within the body can stem from such things, as the body strives to protect itself, and in turn can be translated outwardly into sorrow and distress. But when I grieve now I seem to cry only for a general sense of loss and change that encompasses as much the present and my prospects for the future as it does the past. I sometimes wish it were for something more specific, some hard fact I could focus on and exorcize – a particularly bad hour in theatre, the laborious resecting, something touch-and-go, a vital incision, the feel of dead, matted tissue. Can anaesthetic obliterate so much?

Some months later, when by invitation I attended a lecture on the rarity of my case at Charing Cross Hospital in front of seventy or eighty doctors linked by closed-circuit TV with other doctors at Westminster, I saw slides of necrotic bowel, rotten and severed. It appeared suddenly, without warning, as images thrown large on the screen in front of me. All I could think of was how it resembled grilled Cumberland sausage. I was fascinated but not involved. I was just part of the audience. It didn't seem to have anything to do with me. It didn't upset me. When I try to get close to those moments in theatre, all that I seem to be left with are the birds, the hummingbirds, that were painted on the ceiling of the anaesthetist's room. They were always the last thing I saw. Birds and tropical trees against a blue sky. The black oxygen mask was cupped back and forth over my mouth, my lungs rising and falling, and then the anaesthetic was administered. Wide awake, as I was on later trips to theatre, I'd start the count to ten, convinced the dose was wrong and that I wouldn't go under. And every time I'd go instantaneously, as though a hypnotist had clicked his fingers.

'One, two . . .'

Hummingbirds, hummingbirds.

'. . . three, four, fi . . .'

Gone.

Tracey and my mum shared a relatives room opposite the unit. My mum would come in and see me around seven, after the drug round was over. Her entrances were always measured and well timed – the buzz on the unit's intercom; a slow, soft step across the floor in soft, flat shoes. (I got to recognize her tread, and Tracey's too, and could distinguish them from those of nurses and doctors.) She would arrive gracefully, kiss my forehead or sometimes my feet, hand me a newspaper, and then sit on a low table by the window with the *Daily Mail*, all seemingly in one long, slow sweep. She would always ask me how I had slept, and I hated to answer truthfully and say 'badly' because that would shift the sympathy straight on to me too early in the day, when sometimes all I wanted was a sweet hello on equal terms without acknowledgement of victim and sympathizer.

Sometimes, later in the day, after a bad moment when I'd suffered pain, she would get up from her customary position at the foot of the bed, move closer, and take my hand and rub her thumb along the back of it, her palms thick and warm. Even in those moments I felt incomprehensible to her, as though even then, as her little boy again, I was a closed book, too long unread, the main characters forgotten or misremembered.

I sensed her willing back time, to have a few moments of my childhood all over again, to be of use, to be able to call the school and say I wasn't coming in today, or to fetch my favourite food. I felt we were both on unfamiliar ground, her stroking my hand, mother and child again in outward appearance, but each with our minds full and confused. We were often mute and uneasy in each other's company.

28 January 1962. Eight weeks old. Benjie sleeps from teatime and has to be woken by damp, pulsating, anxious mother at 3 a.m. Very talkative and gurgling after feed. Waves his arms and 'sees' my hand for the first time. There was a week when I rang the doctor to ask if his constant clean nappies were worth worrying about. He still sleeps in his Karry-Kot, as it is still cold. I wash him in the washing-up bowl because of the frozen pipes. Put him out into the perishing but sunny garden today in cap (knitted by me) which could 'do with an inch' as my mother said. M&S mittens. Muffled like a baby Eskimo. He needs fattening up. He has only been gaining a few ounces. When he was born from the first he seemed very contented. Brought into the ward morning and evening, the sun poured on to his cot and he rarely had to be banished to the night nursery. His eyes at birth were dark blue, his hair sparse and mid-brown. His eyebrows were indistinguishable, his lashes long, and his complexion was pale. (From my mum's notes when I was born)

In the relatives room she chose to sleep on the floor, even though Tracey offered her the bed. I think it was some kind of penance. She claimed she slept well, but at night she would retire at about 9.30, leaving Tracey a final hour in the shadows by my bed. When Tracey finally left me and crept into the

37

darkened room, she told me my mum's voice would sound from floor level: 'I'm still awake.' She'd taken to smoking cheap filter cigarettes to calm herself, only to stub them out after a couple of puffs. She searched for order and understanding all the time, tidying up after Tracey, rearranging, changing outfits during the day, making the beds and little piles of things, getting me to repeat things that doctors had said so she could write down key words to remind herself and use to people on the phone. I found her overview of my illness was patchy. Tracey said she told her some facts several times. Her version as relayed to my dad must have been in turns strange, dramatic, true, nonsensical. And yet, above this turmoil and the wrestling with herself, I thought she still managed to present an image of restraint and togetherness by my bedside, and was able to be funny, and to laugh at her attempts to impose order on her confusion. One morning she told me how, from the window of the relatives room, she had devised an ingenious system to hang her washing out over the Horseferry Road, using two wire coat-hangers, and how she was sleeping with her feet in a waste-paper basket to stop the bedclothes from lying on them and making them so hot that it would keep her awake, worrying.

If she felt she was in the way of a test or a drug round she would creep away, and her quiet deference to Tracey in the times when I needed comforting must have been hard for her to sustain sometimes, but the positions around the bed were defined early on, with Tracey at my pillow, my mum at the foot. She despaired at my dad's inability to cope with the proximity of my death. She hated him for it — resented that she was suffering and he wasn't there to share the burden with her, to hold her hand, to be at her pillow. Tracey told me she would come off the phone to him and would shout and storm around the relatives room, tearing her hair with the unfairness of it all. She would travel back to Oxford by train once or twice a week for forty-eight hours, to check, as she said, 'he hadn't fallen in the river' (one of her long-standing fears, when he was drinking) and try to talk to him, put him to bed when he couldn't stand up straight, and be with him. But all the time I know she just longed for his support.

Some nights my half-sister Jennie would come after work, catching the tube up from Richmond. Not that she wouldn't have come anyway, but I think she used to come for Mum's benefit too. She knew the situation in Oxford. She was someone else for my mum to talk to. Mum would bring her in, and as I caught her eye as she came across the room she would cock her head to one side and smile poignantly and ruefully at me, uncomplicated, selfless. They'd sit together at the end of the bed, Jennie always convinced she was sitting on something important or too close to a piece of hospital equipment, and when she'd finally finished shuffling and scratching around she'd settle like a hen on a nest and beam at me. My role as her little brother came out strongly to her. She was nine when I was born. A baby for a little girl. She used to regularly bandage me in pretend games of doctors and nurses. I don't really remember what we talked about when she came to the hospital. I just see her face – happy, sad, engaged, bound up in the immediacy of the present.

★

I am sitting out in a chair today. The sun has just appeared from behind the tall trees outside and is shining on my face through the high windows. The windows are open. I feel air. I close my eyes. I can't believe I am in here, in this place. Hospital. Intensive Care. With my eyes closed I could be in the garden at home or on a beach, but I know when I open them again I won't be so I'll keep them shut for a few more minutes. I am sweating into my dressing-gown, but I don't care.

'Your turn,' says Tracey.

I open my eyes. The Scrabble board is on the invalid-table in front of me.

'Sorry.'

Tracey began with 'ACQUIRE'. I could only manage 'RAT' in response. She is now forty-five points ahead. I have no energy to think. My mind feels like it is running on a run-down battery. When I try to think it turns over like a car engine after the headlights have been left on all night. My neck is stiff. My shoulders hang like the yoke on underfed cattle. This is the furthest we have got with this game. The last two attempts ended in my conceding after only three words. Yesterday I couldn't even face starting, so exhausting was the laying out of the board. Match abandoned. My mum is watching us. She is happier today with my colour. Not so waxy and yellow apparently. I stare at my tiles. Nothing. 'S . . . N . . . I . . U . . .' Wait a minute. SEQUINS! Incredible. I plant the tiles on the board and beam at Tracey.

'What's that?' she asks.

'Sequins. And a double-word score. Thirty-two points.' I am beside myself.

'OK then.' She looks suspicious, but under the circumstances understandable leniency prevails.

40

'Are you all right?' she asks.

The moment exhausts me. 'Yes. But I'm going to have to retire now. Good word though.'

Like a lone diver among sharks, I would watch the cool-eyed doctors and anaesthetists glide round my bed. The doctors on ITU were strange, humourless, intent. They struck me as total scientists – more so than any other doctors I came across. Most of the patients they were treating were living on the slope of death. Patient survival was rooted in the minute analysis of charts and the balancing of chemicals, not so much in warmth of human contact, and so the doctors glided from flickering monitor to flickering monitor amid the sonars of bleeps and alarms, gauging, estimating, quiet, serious. I never struck up a conversation with one of them, just gleaned a few facts and watched them mutter among themselves.

Of course I didn't eat. I was hooked up to a special feeding system called Total Parenteral Nutrition (TPN). Prepared in sealed laboratories by scientists in space suits, the food was a nutritionally balanced, calorie-controlled milkshake, lasting twenty-four hours and costing £250 a bag, fed by a regulated pump directly into my bloodstream via the deep line sunk into my chest called a Hickman line. This was all in order to bypass my digestive system. Each bag was made up specially for every patient who needed one. In spite of being fully intravenously hydrated by an additional saline drip, I instinctively wanted more water. My lips would stick together, and the drugs left bitterness and mustiness in my mouth. Anything passing from my stomach to my intestine, however, would have stimulated dangerous digestive muscle action in the healing gut. Twice a day I was allowed to suck on an ice-cube – I anticipated its arrival like an addict – but only after a naso-gastric tube had been passed up my nose, down the back of my throat and down into my stomach to siphon it off once I'd swallowed the tiny amount of water it gave up. The tube, which was regularly replaced, would tickle when I spoke, as if I were touching the back of my mouth with the tip of my finger.

Henry, an old man opposite me, slept all the time, unhappy on his respirator, beyond the tree line of consciousness for hours on end. When he woke he couldn't speak, and would toss his head around on the pillow. One nurse told me that he'd lost the will to live and often wouldn't even try to breathe, needing reprimands and chest massages. He'd let the female nurses wash him but he'd never let them shave him. I wondered what he was thinking in all those hours of tossing and sighing, stubbly, insistent, stubborn.

All the patients on ITU had X-rays. Every day. Chest X-rays for everyone, and the occasional abdominal X-ray for me. The fear of chest infection was a real one among the nurses and doctors – weakened patients, lying down for days and days, had phlegm massing up around their lungs, havens for bacteria and viruses. The descent into pneumonia or septicaemia can be sudden and fatal. The mobile X-ray machine would come round in the middle of the morning, like a small armoured vehicle, manned by young, brusque female technicians wearing white nylon dresses and lead aprons. I would be sat as upright as possible and rested back against the hard square boards of film, and then shot from above with a lead pad over my groin, while all the nurses went and hid around the corner. 'X-ray,' the technician would cry, and everyone would drop what they were doing and scuttle to a safe distance, until the same voice would cry, 'Breathe in . . . Hold . . . Thank you', and with the all-clear sounded everyone would leave their shelter and pick up their conversations in mid-sentence. Some days I'd be in pain and would be unable to sit up and the nurses would roll me over half-sideways and force the film under the mattress, then roll me back and shoot from overhead. By lunch-time the films were back and processed, snapped up under the clips on the sodium light-box. I got to recognize mine from the dark outline of the negative. After a moment's scrutiny one of the doctors would turn to me and say, 'Clear as a bell.' They all used the same line.

After the morning X-ray round came the physiotherapists – women again, this time in white nylon tunics, mildly flared blue trousers and trainers. The impression given was slightly girls-school sporty. They seemed to bring an atmosphere of hearty fitness with them, marching in, carrying clipboards. It always seemed humorously out of place. Bright, insistent, manipulative, they were keen to get everyone on their feet as soon as possible. I was amazed at how soon I was expected to walk.

It was the first time I really noticed by body. My legs. The weight loss and the muscle depletion. I couldn't believe it. So sudden. I was over twelve stone when I was admitted, and now my legs were like those of a famine victim. I was a fat little boy when I was growing up. Photographs show me unhappy with myself. I wore T-shirts to swim in on holiday, because I didn't like people to see me, and as a teenager when I bought new clothes I forced myself into trousers one size too small so that the girls who worked in the shop wouldn't think I was unattractive. During my twenties I often dieted to lose half a stone. Crash diets for four weeks. I went jogging at university to lose weight when I started going out with Tracey. I went jogging when we started having our photographs taken when we left. I battled constantly with my own self-image. On good days I saw myself as a young Orson Welles; on bad days I was Doughnut from *The Double Deckers*. But now the skin seemed to hang off my arse in little folds, dry and loose. Tracey says I looked like a little old gnome. I'd lost a stone and a half in less than a fortnight. I was just staring at my kneecaps. Huge kneecaps like pool balls. I shuffled to the door of the unit and back, pushing two drip-stands, clutching them like shepherds' crooks. I was hunched over with dreadful backache. The journey there and back was about thirty feet, but it left me feeling tired and sick, wanting to lie down. They made me sit in the chair for a while to keep my circulation going and to keep my chest upright. I had to take deep breaths in front of them and then make myself cough in spite of the intense pain it caused in my stomach.

I had permanent backache. I had my mattress changed two or three times in the first couple of weeks and would sometimes lie with a hand-towel under the small of my back. Sometimes I made the nurses change it just because I was in a foul mood and it gave me something to think about. They were always patient and understanding, tolerant of my irrationality. Most of the time I was on a special air mattress that helped prevent bedsores by evenly distributing the body weight. As my weight dropped and my muscle wasted I felt my bones beneath the skin. They seemed skeletal and unprotected. My pelvis felt like a hard shell. My toenails softened and were hard to cut, and my feet would dry out and the skin would flake. One afternoon, Melanie, a sister on the unit who practised aromatherapy, massaged my feet with oils. It seemed very luxurious. They smelt of grapefruit all afternoon.

The next Sunday morning one of the nurses asked if I'd like a shower. I hadn't washed properly for nearly two weeks. It seemed impossible, like the trip outside just after my operations, but she disconnected me from my feeds and temporarily capped off all the other lines with bungs and stoppers, sat me in a wheelchair, and taped a black bin-liner around my left arm as a makeshift to keep it dry. She draped a dressing-gown around my shoulders and we set off for the shower-room. The wheelchair had a hard seat. It wasn't actually a wheelchair but a commode on wheels with the lid down. We rattled along. I sat very still. I felt like a statue being moved for an exhibition. A couple of nurses waved at me.

There was a plastic chair in the shower-stall. The nurse, Carolyn, held my arm as I stood up. I was wobbly. I let the dressing-gown fall to the floor and stood naked for a moment. I remembered being in there during my time on Marie Céleste. It seemed like years ago. Carolyn turned the water on. I stepped in and sat on the chair. The sensation was overpowering.

45

I am under a waterfall. It is so warm. I can feel my body. It is waking from a deep slumber. The water pounds on my head. I feel lethargy rising and leaving me. My body is singing to me. I feel content for the first time in weeks. I feel like a rare animal saved from extinction. I am tiny. A marsupial. The dressing on my belly is soaking through. Is that OK? The lint and the gauze are wet now. Underneath there are twenty-eight shining staples. I know that. I asked the surgeon. They are holding me together. Not stitches, staples. Do they use a staple gun? My groin is stained with iodine. Amber and copper stains like leaking central-heating pipes. Little rivulets are running down my waterproofed arm. The air smells of blocks of cheap white soap, like school showers. I can catch the water in my bottom lip and spit it out like a whale. I don't want to come out.

Back in my bed in laundered sheets, dusted in talcum powder, my hair still damp, new dressing, I felt like a king. My mum brought my dad to see me that lunch-time. It was the first time I'd seen him since he'd left me in X-ray. He shuffled around a bit, stood out on the balcony while my mum threw glances of apology at me. I found myself treating him as though he were the patient, politely asking after the dog, Grandma and the car, trying to keep the minutes from dipping into silence.

I felt so clean and content in my bed that the awkwardness of the occasion didn't register as much disappointment with me as it did with my mum, whose final look of despair as she led him out touched me more. I'm sure their inability to share their fears was miserable for both of them – my dad deep in a world of denial, speechless and unhappy, drinking heavily; my mum willing to confront it all head on, desperate to understand and to talk to someone. On the day I first went up to theatre and the true seriousness of my illness finally became apparent she had been alerted by Sheila and phoned for a taxi and paid the driver fifty quid to take her all the way from Oxford to London while my dad stayed behind, staring out at the river on his own, his car in the garage, his dog by his side.

21.00–0.700 Night nursing staff start duty. Observation and treatment is geared to providing maximum sleep and rest for the patient during the night-time. (ITU Relatives Leaflet)

The late evenings were long. One night I asked John, one of the staff nurses on the unit, if he'd care to wheel the TV over and watch the midnight cricket highlights with me with the sound down, so as not to disturb the other patients. I was covered in a rash from an allergic reaction to one of the drugs, and the calamine lotion that one of the nurses had been applying all day had started to cake and suddenly it made the itching and irritation worse. In the end, I sat watching the cricket while John stripped the sheets back and washed me down with cool flannels. I felt decadent – washed down by a man at midnight in the flickering glow of a silent TV.

I am trying to get to sleep. It is late. Who's coughing? What's beeping? It must be half two. I can't twist on to my side. I can only sleep on my side. I've been on my back for sixteen hours. If I put this hand under the pillow maybe I can pull myself over a bit. No, that hurts. I want to put one hand between my knees and roll over. Please. Now then. I'm yawning. A good sign. Come on. Gently now. I'll pull on the bed-frame. Haul myself over. Here we go. These drips and feed lines. They keep snagging. They are like seaweed on the keel

47

of a ship. I give up. I'll just list here awhile, then roll back. That shouldn't hurt.

Sleep came fitfully. I had to ask to be laid down. I couldn't do it myself. If I had them lay me down too early, before I was tired, I would lie and stare at the ceiling, the peeling corners, the remnants of Blu-Tack from Christmas decorations, the slow drip-drip-drip of the drugs hanging above me. The hands of the clock never seemed to move between three and five. On bad nights there was a constant chorus of alarms and bleeps from the other beds, or the raised voices of temporary Australian agency nurses coping with a patient's incontinence or Henry's reluctance to breathe through his respirator. An emergency beside another bed could last an hour. I'd lie stock still and listen to forty minutes of 'Come on, now. You can do it. That's it. Good girl. Easy does it.' I'd call someone over and ask to be sat up for no other reason than to be sat up, and then have to be laid down again for no other reason than to be laid down, all the time listening to the quiet chatter of the night staff as they ate apples and chocolate brought from the machine down in reception. They'd talk about *Hello!*, holiday plans, boyfriends; file their nails with emery-boards, prepare drugs. There was a nurse from New Zealand called Marie. On my first night out of sedation, having been told I couldn't eat or drink, I watched her eating peach slices and strawberries from a Tupperware box. I was hot, bone dry. Others were snacking on crisps and Diet Coke, but it was the fruit I suddenly desperately craved. It seemed so wet and real amid the machines and the sonar beeps and the smell of iodine and musky skin.

Images of food and favourite meals started coming to me

regularly. I thought of Saturday mornings growing up, when everyone was still largely living at home. My mum and dad would finish the shopping and then pop down to the pub for an hour. My dad would have prepared his pools coupon, and my mum would have had a little bet on some horses picked solely for their loose connections with the names of members of the family – Simon Says, Ben Nevis, Romany Way – and at two o'clock they'd come home for lunch and an afternoon in front of the TV. Sausages, beans and mash were served around 2.30. When my half-brothers were in their late teens and early twenties they took weekend jobs as bar staff at the same pubs my mum and dad frequented, and sometimes all of them would come home and up to fifteen or twenty sausages could be cooking in the pan at one time. There would be racing from Chepstow or bob-sleigh or all-in wrestling, and the smell all over the flat would be dense and meaty, the wooden spoons stained deep orange with bean sauce, the rising steam from the boiling potatoes misting up the kitchen windows so they'd have to be opened even on the coldest days. On days when a lot of us were home we'd have to take turns in mashing.

I saw garlic-sausage sandwiches made from fresh seeded bloomer that I ate day after day as a schoolboy with glasses of cold milk, the roast lamb and onion sauce for homecomings, the porterhouse steaks for very special occasions when I was the lone teenager at home after everyone else had left, the Hungarian goulash for visitors. I saw foods on the shelf in the meter cupboard in the hall that I have never touched since – Carnation milk, corned beef, luncheon meat, cock-a-leekie soup, prunes, fishpaste. As a thirteen-year-old I considered my ideal moment to be eating a quarter-pound cheeseburger and chips with Devil's Food Cake to follow while seated in a box at Chelsea with Joanna Lumley.

My hospital bed was by the window – old French windows that opened on to a small balcony with a black iron railing. The night nurses would leave the door ajar at night with the tatty green blind pulled down halfway so I could see out. I liked to feel the night breezes on my face, and the door would stay open until another patient complained of a draught or the rattling blind made too much noise. The room overlooked a garden – the public garden I'd walked round on that first Sunday – an umbrella of tall and leafy trees, council flower-beds and a tarmac path. During the day it served as a short cut for most people. Few stopped off to sit on the benches, only drinkers and solitary people. On sunny lunch-times the grassy lawns attracted builders and secretaries.

On one balmy evening the Prof turned from reading my wall chart, jingling the loose change in his pockets, to point out that the tree nearest the balcony must be a fruiter. Spindly and indistinct though it was, he said it was plum. He took his holidays in Kent. Nobody could disagree with him. He was a charmer who wore bird's-eye-check suits in a style reminiscent of the ones my dad had made in the sixties when he was Jack-the-Lad on Archer Street. I think my mum quite fancied the Prof – white swept-back sideburns, little veins on his cheeks and nose, twinkly, relaxed. He had an air of maverick authority about him. An irresistible quality to my mum.

At night the garden was different. The pub on the far side looked neo-thirties, and after hours the awning lights were left on, casting a soft orangey light over the streets. Cars would glide by. Garage doors would open and close at 3 a.m. Figures on the pavements. Leaf shadows dancing on the blind. It made my life seem cinematic and even more extraordinary than it already was.

There were two corner rooms on the unit, separated from the main room by glass windows. Serious cases in need of complete isolation went in them. Henry was in one for a couple of nights. A young black girl was put straight into the other when she arrived. All her skin was coming off, like the pith of an orange. I saw blisters and ulcers all across her face. She'd had a bad reaction to a drug. The nurses smothered her in creams and jellies to try to hold her together. Her family came in regularly and brought her cassettes to listen to. She couldn't speak. Her mouth and lips were all affected. I caught sight of her occasionally. She was always sitting upright, day or night. Music seeped from her room – Anita Baker, Luther. When the doctors came to see her the blinds were pulled down.

I dreaded being confronted with other people's pain. I dreaded a moment in the night when the doors would be flung open and a crash victim would be brought in. I imagined blood and panic, the 'wild white face' of Larkin's 'Ambulances'. Of course all that would have happened already in Accident & Emergency and by the time they'd been sent up to ITU they would have looked like every other patient – sedated, ventilated, on their backs, hidden under clean white cotton blankets – but I still watched the doors at night.

I listened for the alarms chiming like cookers and digital watches from the other beds. I got used to their patterns and didn't like it if they went off irregularly. I watched the faces of the nurses if they picked up the phone or took one another aside.

I sometimes blocked my ears with my fingers when curtains were drawn round other beds. Someone came to fit a drip into Gwen's arm late one night. Gwen was very old and tiny like a bird, and her bowel was twisted. She spoke so kindly to everyone in her quiet high fluty voice. She greeted everyone who came to her not with a 'Hello' but with a statement of her age and the number of great-grandchildren she had. She had real grey hair, not permed or colour-rinsed, but shoulder length and in shades of real grey and steel and silver. She had no bad words to say. I knew the drip fitting would be painful and I had seen her small thin arms. But when the voice said 'Hold still' I really couldn't bear to listen to her sharp gasps and gentle cries of shock and pain. They were like high, soft, falling scales of melody. It made my own anguish seem so boorish.

I could never tell if anyone actually died on the unit while I was on it. Tracey says a man – a frightening, skeletal scarecrow of a man – died of anorexia during my first week, but I never saw him. I always half-expected to see priests in frockcoats and solemnity, the closing of the eyelids, a sheet pulled over the head; but if anyone did die it was handled discreetly, and if they were quietly disconnected from their life-support rigs and wheeled away it was done behind curtains and made to look like any other trip up to theatre.

★

It was ten days after my last bowel-resection operation before I was allowed to drink anything. Of course I was well hydrated with a drip and the Hickman line feeding me TPN, but my mouth would crave liquid. Other than the occasional ice-cube, I was sometimes allowed to suck on a tiny pink sponge, about the size of a sugar lump, dipped in water, to wet my mouth.

On the tenth day I began drinking thimblefuls of water every couple of hours. Every day from then on, the Prof would come round and listen to my abdomen with his stethoscope for signs of life. 'Bowel sounds' were an indication of the body readjusting and beginning to work again. For a long time there was nothing. The Prof would look up and say, 'Hmmm . . . pretty quiet in there', and the surgeons gathered round my bed would shuffle off, murmuring and muttering. They were never introduced, although as a group they had kinder faces than the unit's anaesthetists.

Of course the subject of food came up. I stunned my mum on only my second day on ITU by asking her, by way of my first serious question, whether I would still be able to eat well. She was speechless. At that stage nobody knew whether I was going to be on a drip for the rest of my life. I used to push the Prof on the matter. He said it was hard to say, but if things didn't get worse I would possibly be able to eat lean meat and rice, thin soups and little portions of ice-cream. He asked if I liked jelly and custard. Blancmange.

He said most people had between twelve and fifteen feet of small intestine in which to do their digesting. He had managed to save me just under three feet. He reassured Tracey one night by telling her there were some people out there surviving with less. The constant trips up to theatre that I had endured were in part an attempt to save as much of the gut as possible, to only take out precisely what was necessary. Every inch saved was critical if I was going to recover and then have a relatively normal life. I've since been told that a less experienced surgeon when confronted with my rotting gut could quite easily have panicked and taken the whole lot out entirely that first day, leaving me a permanent hospital life to look forward to, never eating again, plumbed into a drip-feed.

When my bowel did finally start to move I felt like a child learning potty-training all over again. The commode would be wheeled in and I'd sit on it, passing what looked more like seagull shit than anything I could recognize. I'd fill up with pockets of gas, which when released on the unsuspecting unit would resound off the stainless-steel bowl like rifle shots, leaving me sniggering like a schoolboy behind the curtain pulled around my bed.

At least I never had trouble urinating. I got the nurses to take the catheter out as soon as possible, and one of my greatest pleasures during all my time in hospital was taking the plastic urine bottles into the bed and pissing, lying half-upright under the warm bedclothes – rich, hot, mustardy piss, strong in the odour of chemicals and drug residues.

A Greek Island. I am thirteen. There is a donkey by the road – a road of dry baked soil, thorns and scrub. There is no shade as far as the eye can see except for the fig-tree the donkey is standing under. The donkey is urinating. His cock hangs flaccid like a small elephant's trunk, gently swaying back and forth in the silent heat. A thick, loose, endless stream washes into the dust. I stare. It is amazing to me. His thing. He is so casual. So relaxed. Chewing on figs. Hosing down the road. I want to be that donkey.

The Prof went away on his holidays shortly after. Kent. I always pictured flat sunny days, oast-houses and apple orchards, the Prof in cotton slacks in a garden somewhere. Gins on the lawn. I had been started on capfuls of Fortisip, a build-up potion that smelled like 3-IN-ONE bicycle oil. Nick Law, his senior registrar, took charge for a week, but when, on a Sunday morning, I was suddenly stricken with a new, awful, abdominal pain, he was not on duty and a hurried call was put in to the weekend emergency surgeon, Mr Hunter.

I was sitting on the edge of the bed. It was quite early, around 7.30. Tracey had been woken by one of the nurses and had come in from the relatives room to be with me. I was hunched over with excruciating pain, naked except for a towel over my shoulders. I'd tried to get up for an imaginary shit and had nearly fainted. The message came back from Mr Hunter that he would be as quick as he could, but he was, ironically, waiting in for an emergency plumber.

'Me too,' I managed to say to one of the nurses.

A little while later he arrived. He rolled me over, gave me a prod up the arse, rolled me back, tapped and fingered my belly, said we should 'sit tight', and ordered pethidine, a morphine substitute. I took a heavy jab in my thigh and felt the muscle harden as the fluid rushed into my system. The drug was intense, protective, insulating. Within minutes I felt sleepy and wildly intoxicated. I drifted. The pillow seemed to swallow up my head, and for four hours I sank and resurfaced over and over again, warm, untroubled, on my own wide sea, the pain supported and cradled in the soft currents.

I imagined I was on Bird Island in the Indian Ocean, in a tropical downpour, the rain as warm as the waves, and I dreamt of the ten days I spent there with Tracey when we were mistaken for a honeymoon couple. I had flowers flown in on Valentine's Day, and we spent the early mornings beachcombing for splintered driftwood and the evenings amid the wheeling frigates and the birds feeding by the water's edge. The tik-tik-tik of whimbrels. Sanderlings and plovers. I found a piece of coral shaped like the tubes leading from a human heart. Darkness dropped like a curtain. We were intensely happy. Wicker hurricane-lamps swung from the terrace outside our room. Tiny crabs scuttled in the wet grass at night, and the moon settled like a giant blood orange on the sea.

Tracey sat by my bed and read. She held my hand, releasing it momentarily every couple of minutes to turn the page, and then taking it again until it felt cold, when she would slip it back under the blankets.

I couldn't begin to think who we were becoming or if we were the same any more. Everything was in a sharply focused present. There was no past to us I could recognize or wanted to compare. No future either. I saw a repeated image of her walking by the Embankment alone, just walking to fill time, the right foot barely knowing what the left was doing, and it left me speechless. Many hours passed in silence, as though we were saying in code, 'I know. I know. Later, later.'

I took two more painkilling jabs that day and don't recall

any more. By the Monday morning the pains had subsided a little, Nick Law was back, and there was talk of another investigative trip to theatre. It was decided to remove the Hickman line from my chest. The site where the line entered my chest had become vulnerable to infection, and under the circumstances it was considered a wise precaution to remove it. I would be fed through my arms instead and another Hickman would be inserted in a couple of days.

That evening the anaesthetist arrived to take it out under a local anaesthetic while I lay in bed. They said I was too vulnerable to infection to be taken off the unit. Needles were becoming a phobia. They tried applying numbing creams before starting, but I still started to wriggle. The local was jabbed into my chest. Two nurses had to hold me down as the anaesthetist leant over and cut the skin that had grown around the site of the line. A stitch was holding the line in place and had to be cut away. Tracey was just saying 'Look away. Look away' over and over again.

The line was drawn slowly from my chest. It must have been fed in at least a foot. I wanted to yank it and finish it off myself. When it was over they put me in the chair and tried to calm me down. I was taking shallow, shocked breaths. They told me they had to take some blood to use for cultures. My veins were small and useless. The needle drew nothing from either arm and I shouted out and tried to get up. It was finally jabbed into my knuckle.

By the next morning things had improved and I was given a reprieve. The trip to theatre was cancelled. The pains were never really explained.

★

57

Since the shot of cyclophosphamide after my first operation, I'd effectively been left with a severely depleted immune system. The drug simply erases large amounts of white cells and then waits for the body to re-establish them over a few days, hopefully at a normal level again – like switching off a TV and then turning it on again hoping for the picture to settle. However, the drug does not differentiate between normal infection-fighting white cells and the troublesome allergy-response cells. I was wide open to any passing bugs and bacteria.

I had regular mouthwashes and antifungal rinses. Everyone had to wash their hands before coming in to see me. Tracey and my mum were discouraged from kissing me goodnight. My mum took to kissing my foot or my forehead. Tracey was allowed to help wash my hair, fixing a shallow tray under my head at the end of the bed with a special drain-hole that emptied into a bucket placed on the floor. Hair-washing was quite a treat. I loved the massaging, the physical contact, the sensuality, the smell of baby shampoo, the damp drying hair. My hair was washed and my blood continued to be taken every day.

For ten days my blood results were scrutinized daily for signs of infection or the eosinophil count restabilizing itself. Nurses would phone down to the labs at lunch-time, or a porter would bring in the pink piece of paper with the results. It was like waiting for a lottery result. My infection-fighting cells returned to normal as expected, but my eosinophils initially overshot their normal mark when they began appearing again, and every one feared the worst – that they were signalling the immune system's continuing volatility and instability – but two days later they started to fall again and then stabilized at just above normal. It was a good sign. People began to talk of me moving on to one of the wards to begin a full healing process.

Samples of my bowel had been taken for tissue-analysis tests for a fuller diagnosis. The rheumatologists were suspecting a particular rare form of autoimmune disease but were diplomatically using a temporary generic description – eosino-philic vasculitis – while the definitive tests were undertaken by the histologists. It looked likely, however, that my immune system had responded to some kind of allergy, not a parasite or virus.

Less vulnerable to infection, I was allowed out in a wheel-chair again – I'd been 'off games' for a few days – and Tracey would push me across the corridor into the room where she and my mum were staying, and we would sit for an hour and watch the Barcelona Olympics on a portable TV. Mum would have had a little tidy-up especially, and Tracey would make them a cup of tea and we would all try to treat it as a kind of visit, striking up conversations with renewed enthusiasm even though we'd all been in each other's company across the corridor only minutes before.

Two days later I was told that I was finally going to be moved upstairs to St Mark's, a surgical recovery ward. I didn't want to go. I envisaged a long Nightingale ward, men coughing all night and a TV on all day, afternoon dead-time quiz shows playing to inattentive, listless watchers, trolleys of inedible food.

When the day came, I was to go via theatre, where a fresh Hickman line was to be inserted in my chest under general anaesthetic to enable me to be fed by TPN again. I'd had two days of emergency temporary food drips in my wrists. My arms had stung and buzzed with the strain of thick, gritty fluids.

I joined a stacking system. Hickman lines were obviously not top of the list, as my slot was shifted back from late morning. It was 4.30 by the time I eventually left the unit. I remember sitting on the edge of the trolley for an hour, waiting for the porters to come and get me. The unit was full of sunshine. The green trees of the gardens were behind me. I dangled my legs over the side, gently swinging them to and fro. I felt like a child on a bunk-bed. I was wearing a cotton theatre robe, stiff and starched, tied in bows down the back. Everybody I saw who wore one standing up felt their arse was on show and that everyone else was looking. I used to watch wide-eyed out-patients and newcomers, sometimes up at X-ray or preparing for theatre, pulling the material together behind them, covering up, grasping at their dignity. Theatre gowns are a cruel design, playing on the quiet humiliation brought on by unfamiliar hospital life. They level everyone. Hospital turns life upside down. It seems fitting that the uniform should be a gown worn back to front.

The steel trolley frame was cold against the back of my thighs. All my lines had been removed, even my temporary feeding lines. I felt relaxed. Up on the top floor, the theatre floor, I was wheeled into the anaesthetist's room. The black cup came. I breathed in the oxygen. The veins in my arms were dry river-beds and I had no lines, so the needle for the anaesthetic had to be twice jammed in deep before the blood-table was found. It felt like a big needle. In my mind's eye I saw oilrigs, derricks out at sea, the huge spinning drills spitting oil, churning, billowing waves, grey and green, the colours of nausea, men in hard hats tapping deep into the core of the earth, below the sea floor. I winced and flinched as the needle was held in. The anaesthetist mumbled behind his mask. I closed my eyes.

'One, two . . .'

Hummingbirds, hummingbirds.

'. . . three, four, fi . . .'

Gone.

THREE

I am lying on my side. Why my side? Who rolled me over? The cotton blanket is warm. The trolley is hard. I am frightened to move lest I disturb the surgeon's work. Or cause pain. Fresh, crisp, newly made pain. The light is bright and even and white all over the room. It is like opening a fridge door. A nurse sits at a table. Other trolleys. Other sleeping patients on their sides. Not many. I can see two. I am thirsty. I think I want to shit. I move a little. A little test. My chest hurts. I stop moving. I close my eyes and press my nose into the cotton blanket. Rest and sleep. A good place. Save me. Recuperation has a soft rhythm. My heart beats. I can feel the blood in my eyelids. The air from my nostrils is hot in the bedclothes against my face. My knees feel hard, stacked one above the other. I curl one big toe over the other. Gently. My feet are friends. I see our house. Papers all over the bed. The smell of matting in the hall when I come back from being away. Voices now. Someone laughs. I open my eyes again. How long did I drift? Two minutes? Two hours? The nurse has seen me. She calls the porters. I am in the recovery room.

St Mark's. The porter has gone. My chest hurts. The new Hickman is in. On the other side this time. I have a little suture where the old one was. It is early evening. I have a bed in the corner. The ward is quietly buzzing. I am unused to such activity. Visitors, lowered voices. There are a lot of flowers. Flowers weren't allowed in ITU. Bugs in

62

the water. There is a young couple opposite. He is in the bed; she holds his hand. He looks my age. He wears blue pyjamas and pulls a face when he moves. He has soft-drink bottles on his bedside table. Everybody does. Robinson's, Ribena. My pillows are at an uncomfortable angle. My back aches and my chest is sore. I can't be bothered to move. The air seems close. Tracey is next to me. My mum next to her. A staff nurse arrives. She is quick around the bed, slightly sharp in her manner. She is young, with the manner of a school prefect. Blood pressure, temperature, pulse. She asks me to sit up. I say I can't. She says, 'Try.' I say I haven't been able to sit up on my own for three weeks. She says I have to. 'This isn't ITU any more. This is the road to recovery.' Another nurse comes over. They slip their arms under my armpits and each puts one knee on the bed. 'Sit forward.' I try. My stomach muscles don't respond. It hurts. I am fuggy from the anaesthetic. They heave me forward. I cry out. They hold me there. I am limp, like a puppy in its mother's mouth, but there is dreadful, dreadful pain. So bad, I have no breath. I can't draw in breath to speak. I open and close my mouth like a fish. I want to stay, 'Stop.' One syllable, and I can't say it. Nobody knows what I want, because I am silent. I am lonely. My pillows are rearranged, my bed-rest altered. One, two, three. They heave me back. I cry out. Tracey is distressed. I smile weakly. I don't want her to worry. She smiles weakly too. At last I am still. The nurses go. They have hung a little plastic sign from the bed frame above my head that says, 'Nil By Mouth'.

That night, my first on St Mark's, the man in the bed next to me was complaining of feeling cold. He'd had prostate surgery, I think. Huge water-bags to flush through his kidneys were hanging at the foot of his bed, with tubes running under the bedclothes. An hour later he was shivering and his teeth were chattering. A nurse brought in a special super-lightweight insulating blanket, like thin Bacofoil, the type we were all told the first astronauts on the moon used. My mum returned from a trip to America around the time of the first Apollo moon landing, and brought one back – silver on one side, gold on the other. I was seven at the time. I used to wrap myself up in it on the sitting-room floor in front of the TV until I got so hot I'd nearly faint. Things like nearly fainting and holding my breath until my lungs almost burst, or shutting myself in a small cupboard until I nearly suffocated, were fascinating to me as a child. At school I used to pierce the skin on the back of my hand with the end of a compass or push the end of a plastic protractor under my fingernails just to find out what it felt like.

The man in the bed next to me rustled under the Bacofoil blanket, and more bedclothes were put on top to hold it down. He asked for the window to be closed. I thought it was stifling.

I tried to take my first solid food for three weeks. Scrambled eggs and a slice of white toast. I didn't really feel hungry but craved the action of eating. I felt fine until the late afternoon, when I began to feel nauseous. My bowels cramped up. I started to vomit – not regular vomit, but watery green bile. I filled a bowl beside my bed. At eight, though, it really started. A whole litre this time. Strangely, it wasn't an unpleasant experience. Quite nice all things considered. I seemed simply to have to open my mouth. The velocity with which the green bile erupted was astonishing, like a geyser. It was fascinating. Like cartoon spewing. I had five or six spasms, with either

Tracey or a nurse passing fresh disposable buckets in the shape of bowler hats to me like firemen, while I filled them up and handed them back down the line.

The next day my mum finally made my dad come up and see me, now that I was off ITU. He drove the two of them up in his new Mazda 323 – 'Laguna Blue with ABS,' he took pride in telling me. It was a Sunday. He was able to park next to the hospital. He hates coming up to town if he can't park safely somewhere. The ward was warm and full of sunlight. Some beds were empty. The hospital tended to discharge people on Friday if it possibly could, to keep the place quiet and just ticking over until Monday morning.

My mum sat at the end of the bed. She had brought a few photos of the family and a newspaper cutting. My dad was quiet and ill at ease, but then I asked him to sit right up near me. I was in quite a lot of discomfort. I suddenly felt sick and ready to vomit again and had to slowly swing my legs out of the bed to sit on the edge and stare into the bucket on the floor. The moment passed. I felt my forehead cool and the blood beat in my face for a minute. My dad came and sat next to me. We sat together with our little legs side by side, and just started talking in quiet voices – nothing demonstrative or loaded with meaning: just odd things about the car, about jazz and the cricket. I felt like we were boys. And I realized that was how he wanted it. He didn't really want to be my grown-up dad. He wanted to be on equal terms, conspiratorial and even-handed. Good fellas. Little musketeers. I told him I liked his shoes, and he said he would get me a pair. It was something concrete that he could do.

When I was growing up he'd always seemed more like me and less like an adult. He used to come and watch me play football for the school under-thirteens team. I'd be in goal. I don't think he liked the company of the other parents and teachers much. He preferred to slope away from the central mass around the halfway line and would end up on his own behind the goal at my end, offering me a square of chocolate through the net. I'd have to shoo him away, because he'd be putting me off. One week he stood there right from the kick-off. I told him to move, but he wouldn't. The opposition kicked off and fed the ball out to the winger, who beat three players, nutmegged the full-back, and chipped me from outside the box. He was only eleven. The ball floated straight over my head and into the net, while I was still half-talking to my dad over my shoulder. One-nil after fifteen seconds. I wouldn't speak to him all day after that, even though we ended up winning 4–3.

I thought of the days he used to take me to football. Saturday afternoons. We never went to Chelsea, although they were my team. I could sense my dad felt uneasy with a big terrace crowd and it made both of us quiet and not able to enjoy ourselves. There was often violence at Chelsea too. Instead we usually took a short drive over to Fulham, where we won the Golden Goals one week. We bought a ticket that had the correct time of the opening goal of the game inside it. Two minutes and two seconds. Fulham 0, Burnley 1. Twenty-five quid we won, collected from the secretary's office after the match. Not only that but we also met Brian Moore behind the stand before the game. I was in heaven. We must have sat in the new Riverside

Stand that day, to try it out. Normally we'd be up at the top of the uncovered end, by the tea-bar, stamping our feet to keep warm. Behind us were the trees of Bishop's Park, and within kicking distance the Thames. The ground is right on the river. I liked the wide sky, the sparkling surface of the water under winter sun, the flocks of starlings against the failing light, the glimpses of scullers and pleasure cruises, the wind swooping through the tall elms. I felt a part of it all but also apart from it all, as though we had been dropped in from outer space to watch the people and the players from a sealed capsule of our own.

Other days we drove all the way out to Charlton. Charlton Athletic were my dad's team. Blackheath was where he first lived when he moved to London. The Valley was a huge ground. Sixty thousand used to go, my dad said. We'd be lucky if five thousand were there whenever we went. The wind would race viciously along the terrace that ran the length of the pitch right from the kick-off, and we'd almost always leave halfway through the second half, frozen stiff. We'd race each other along the back streets to the car, trying to be the first to spot a car with a theft-prevention bar attached to the steering-wheel, at which point whoever had got to it would shout out, 'Krooklok! One–nil!' I looked forward to the journeys home, darkness falling, tail-lights, thickening traffic, results on the radio, smoothing the match programme on my knee, the car heater blowing hot air on my tingling feet, my dad driving. It seemed to have nothing to do with football at all.

Four hours after my mum and dad had gone, another litre of bile came up, and the same again at midnight. It was decided that a new naso-gastric tube should be fed into my stomach to help siphon off the build-up of liquid. The night nurses on duty were young and inexperienced, but were obliged to do the job. It was late. The ward was quiet. It was a miserable ten minutes as the thin pipe was fed up my nose and down the back of my throat and then, mistakenly, twice down into my lungs rather than my stomach, while I retched and coughed, tears streaming down my face. They gave up, pulled the tube out, and said someone else would try in the morning.

Some time later I was woken out of a sleep by the sound of people running. The man under the Bacofoil was convulsing. It was 2 a.m. I tried to sit up. Doctors and nurses were running into the ward. The urgency in their voices frightened me. I heard orders, calm, insistent. Pager alarms were going off. Someone pulled a curtain round my bed so I couldn't see anything. A nurse raced past pushing a machine. I thought I heard them hitting his chest. Hard. Repeatedly. I sat staring at the curtain. I could see people's feet. I wanted to go home. And then the feet stepped away and the bed was sped away. Doctors walked out after it. And then it was quiet. My curtains were pulled back. No one said anything. And it was just quiet. I knew the whole ward was awake, but no one spoke.

The next day a more experienced staff nurse made me drink continuously from a glass of weak lemon barley water while she effortlessly slid my new naso-gastric tube up and down and into place. The swallowing – a neat trick – helped the tube down into the stomach without me having to think about it, and then we all laughed as she pumped out all the lemon I had just drunk. For the next twenty-four hours, whenever I felt nauseous, a nurse would aspirate the tube, drawing the bile out with a large plastic syringe. I would watch it run down the tube from my nose. Sometimes it would be pale and yellow, like finger-bowl water. Other times it would come up thick and green and full of sediment, like pond algae or mint sauce.

I was taken to Ultrasound. I got to like the Ultrasound room, just along from X-ray, with its dim lighting and soft-carpeted floor. It always took me a couple of minutes to move out of the wheelchair and lie down on the hard bed, my knees slightly bent. The jelly that was squeezed on to my stomach was cool and thick. I knew they were looking for an obstruction that could be triggering the vomiting. The hard plastic sensor was run over my belly, digging under my ribs and into my side. On the monitor screen, a million tiny stars appeared in the darkness. As the sensor moved, they changed shape and form and my organs showed up like constellations in the night sky. There was my liver. There was a kidney. There was a big black hole where my gut once was. Another doctor arrived and pointed at the screen.

'Blimey! Not a lot in there.'

'Can you spot his gall-bladder? I can't seem to find it.'

'That's it there. Oh no, wait a minute, that can't be it.'

'That's what I thought. I think it's moved.'

'Well, we can't have that. We can't have a roaming organ.'

After twenty minutes I was wiped down with hard kitchen paper and told to put my pyjama jacket back on. They had found nothing out of the ordinary. Even so, I puked all through the next day again. All food and drink were withheld and a barium meal was booked for nine o'clock the next morning.

★

I am outside the barium room. It is cold in this narrow corridor. I am in a wheelchair. My dressing-grown seems thin and uncomforting. There are two cotton wheelie-bins for laundry next to me. They are both full. One is of white material, the other red. The red one is marked for Aids patients' laundry only. Contents to be incinerated. My gut aches. It is an early start. There is no one else in this corridor. I can hear people behind doors. I have a book to read, but I can't concentrate. I keep seeing the red bin from the corner of my eye. It is so close I could reach out and touch its contents.

I am drinking the barium meal. It comes in a plastic cup. It is heavy and cold. It tastes like chalk-dust and lime. It is thick, undrinkable. I try to swallow it all in one go, but it is too viscous. I just want to put it down. The nurses wait till I have finished it. They stand me up. The wheelchair spins round. I stumble. They hold me up. They slip my dressing-gown off but leave one arm turned inside out and hanging from my drip-stand. The drip in my forearm stops them undressing me fully. I stoop forwards. In front of me there is a steel plate the size of a mattress on its end. I step on to the lip of it and face the room. It is dark. The windows are blacked out. A button is pressed. The steel mattress starts to flip me up slowly. I think of Virgil in Thunderbird 2. I feel the barium in my gullet. It sloops down into my stomach. The mattress stops and they take pictures. The barium shows up on a black-and-white monitor like a thin oil-slick in my digestive tract. I am cold. The doctor is Irish, getting on, I'd say – friendly but concentrated. Suddenly the lights come on. I am led over to a trolley and told to lie down. I ask for an extra blanket.

I am in another room along the corridor. I am half lying on my side. I don't want to be, but I have to stay this way for an hour, to let the barium move down into my gut, when they will take more pictures.

The trolley is hard. No one would hear if I called. Harsh Tannoy
messages blurt into the room, paging doctors, asking technicians to report
to other rooms. It is even less human in here. I think of hamsters and
mice and laboratories.

I get on to another revolving board and have more pictures taken. I
watch the barium on the monitor. On the screen, in negative imaging,
my tiny gut is like a baggy, translucent air duct, fluid, gently moving
like a tired muscle, and in it, showing up black again, are sumps and
puddles of barium. They think there is some kind of obstruction. I will
have to go to theatre again. Maybe Thursday or Friday. Another
operation.

I am defeated.

I went to theatre a couple of days later. I was still vomiting.
Scar tissue and temporary adhesions in my healing intestine
were suspected, stopping the passage of food. The nurses and
staff up on the theatre floors were getting to know me well.
As the lift doors opened and my trolley was wheeled into the
corridor, it was like returning to a familiar hotel.

'Hello, Ben.'

'Are you back again? We can't keep you away.'

'Same room as before, sir?'

When I came round later on that evening I was back on ITU.
It was dark outside. I couldn't focus my eyes. I had another
catheter in, which I resented. It made me feel old, incapable,
incontinent. I had another epidural too. I thought that was
serious. The drug was loaded in its syringe case, mounted on
a drip-stand beside me. There was an immense stabbing pain
in my lower right-hand side every time I moved – very sharp,

and unlike any other pain until then. Tracey was already by my bed.

'They found a huge abscess. Near your bowel,' she said. 'They've drained most of it off, but it was too big and they said you were tiring. That's why you're here.'

I had a drain still in place, a plastic tube running from the site inside, like the straw from a lidded soft-drink beaker, out into a plastic bag lying in the bed. The tube was held in place by a dressing and a thick thread stitched into my belly. My mum was there. The light had gone from outside. Nick Law arrived.

'Well, we didn't expect this,' he said. 'Can't trust those Ultrasound people. Don't know how they missed it. Now we're not sure if it was the cause of all the vomiting or whether another obstruction is still hiding in there, but we thought we'd leave you be for a night. You've been through enough again.'

'Then what?' I asked.

'Well, we can't guarantee that we won't have to go in again, but your bowel is still in a bit of mess from the last time. A bit unstable. Don't want to tamper around too much.'

'What about the drain?'

'Yes, sorry about that. Needed to siphon off the excess. I should tell you, though, it was probably the biggest, smelliest abscess I have ever known.'

'Really?'

'Yup. Size of a cricket-ball.'

After he'd gone, I lay back confused. There was too much new information. So much work undone. I could only think of the days it had set me back. How much longer now? More weeks?

In the first few days on ITU I had kept on asking the doctors and surgeons how much longer. 'A few more days?' I'd say stupidly. 'Surely, no more?' They were patient with me. Tracey knew, I'm sure, that it was going to be a long road. I could only think of getting out. I couldn't register the fact that my life was being threatened, or that I had barely survived the week-long surgery, or that a sweeping infection could strike me down at any moment, or that all the people closest to me were still reeling from the shock of my nearly dying. The future had no complications either: no drips, or tests; no diarrhoea or vomiting; no nausea; no grey-faced pain; no weight-loss or night sweats; no depression, temperature spikes or ambulances; no creeping return of abnormal blood counts, chest pains, aching joints – just a simple rehabilitation and a return to normal.

Ten minutes later my teeth started chattering. I wasn't cold, but the chattering was uncontrollable. It shook my body. The pain in my side was aggravated by every tiny movement. It burned fiercely. I thought of branded cattle. An anaesthetist was called, and he told me it was the effect of the anaesthetic wearing off. It could last several hours. It frightened my mum. He left. I gripped my jaws together, but my torso would shake and sweat. I tried to speak, but the words came out all chopped up and stuttered. An hour later the shaking and chattering stopped. It was like a wind dropping suddenly, and I felt I was looking out over slack fields and damp, leafless trees. It was late. Tracey had to go.

After she left the hospital was quiet. I so wanted to be able to lie on my side, to curl up like a winter animal in its leaves and twigs, somewhere below the earth, to close my eyes and wait till morning, but I couldn't twist at all, and when the nurses tried to lower my bed and lay me flat I had to be sat up again. And that night was perhaps the worst of all: upright, immobile, exhausted, too tired to sleep, the long road up ahead now disappearing into the darkness, and I felt like I was driving all night on an empty single carriageway, nothing in my mirror, the headlights making little impression on the infinite world.

I was stoked up again with steroids and antibiotics. In the morning, Nick Law came round to see me. He was chatty and optimistic. By late afternoon it was decided I should go back up to the ward. I wanted to stay. I still couldn't move without excessive pain and I wanted the extra attention I was getting on ITU, but the doctors were concerned I was vulnerable to infection again and that the ward would be safer, as they had a contagious case on the unit. The epidural was removed and I was taken up that night to St Mark's, to a different bed. I had Voltarol injections in my thigh to kill the pain. I wanted familiarity, but there was none. It was stuffy. The air was like padding. I had the window opened, but the man next to me had it closed again. I slept fitfully, listening out for myself, like a mother anxiously listens out for her baby. In the night I had a shit into a bedpan. Nick Law was thrilled in the morning.

FOUR

There is a red dinosaur on my bedside table. It's a present from Debbie's little kids, James and Richard. They are seven and four, Tracey's nephews. Debbie is Tracey's older sister. They are only two years apart. All four of them have just been to the dinosaur exhibition at the Natural History Museum. I am sitting up in bed. The Prof has returned and put me back to Nil By Mouth. I have a naso-gastric tube back in, but I've got my old bed back again. James and Richard look serious and wide-eyed, a little shocked and quiet and still. They are only young. They have superb thick blond hair and faultless faces. I think of how I must look to them – ancient, drawn, dry and strange. They each have Mutant Ninja Turtle rucksacks. James rummages in his and brings out another present for me – a programme from the England versus Pakistan Lord's test match. He asks me who my favourite player is. Richard keeps looking at the tube in my nose. He is terribly quiet. He offers me a jelly snake. In my croaking voice, I have to tell him I can't eat jelly snakes, and that in fact I can't eat anything just at the moment.

James pipes up. 'Ben, what happened to you?'

I think and try to be concise. 'An illness has attacked my tummy and I have had to have a lot of it removed, but I'm getting better now,' I say.

'Oh.' There is a pause. Then he asks, 'Have you had your lungs removed?'

Tracey and Debbie laugh. They look so alike sometimes.

Ten minutes later Richard is about to offer me another jelly snake, and then I see him remember and he stops himself.

An hour and a half has passed. The four of them have been out and come back. They've been out looking for a riverboat on the Thames. I've been dozing. Richard kept wanting to come back and see that I was all right. He wanted to know if the tube in my nose was hurting me.

In the opposite bed to me was Arnold for a while. He must have been seventy or eighty. He had had a stroke and was suffering prostate trouble. He was unbearably gentle and touching in his manner. He struggled to form words, and was incapable of saying anything except 'Oh, I say!' This was used for all occasions – to express surprise at being hoisted out of bed by hospital porters, delight at the arrival of apple crumble and custard, as a 'Good morning' when I would wave to him after the first ward round of the day. Often the exclamation was combined with a beam and an optimistic thumbs-up. His presence was strangely life-affirming, in spite of the obvious gravity of his condition. It was like having Dan Maskell in the bed opposite.

Patients came and went on the ward. Some men would get restless and fidgety after only two or three days, as they got over operations for piles or prostates. If they racked up ten days they would start to get proud and hardened, thinking they were veterans until they asked me or Kevin down in the end bed how long we had been in.

If I could say five weeks, Kevin could say twelve. Kevin

was thin, with stringy long red hair, and probably only my age or even younger. He had suffered dreadful abscesses in his chest cavity from drug abuse. His eyes were beads in their sockets, intense and shining. The nurses would jack him up with opiate alternatives when the pain got bad, and I would watch him slide off the edge into a reeling, sleep-filled haze for a few hours. His parents would come regularly. They were quiet people, bringing fruit and sweets. On the days before he finally went home, some time later, he shuffled up and down the ward in disposable foam hospital slippers, a purple T-shirt and pyjama trousers, smiling and talking intensely, like he was still wired. The day before he went, the nurses baked him a cake and he had a tiny party in the day-room.

As a group – perhaps only one or two of us talking, while the others in nearby beds listened – a bond would emerge in the periods between ward rounds and visiting times, away from the scrutiny of doctors and the quiet flustering of relatives. The bond's common language was the wink, delivered across the room to the person opposite, as if to say, 'They all think we're ill, but we know we're all right. We're just having them on.'

Bert, opposite me, was a master of the wink, performed in good spirits or under duress. He always seemed to be saying, 'Two pounds of carrots and a bell pepper? I'll see you're all right.'

I casually winked and smiled at a new arrival, Tim, on his first day, as he was being wheeled in from theatre. He was craning his neck and looked nervously around the room. A week later he came over. He picked up a piece of Tracey's jigsaw and fiddled with it. And then he thanked me for winking.

★

Michael, a man from Hornsey, moved into the bed next to me after about a week or so. He had just had major abdominal surgery too. Cancer, I think. It was his second time. Different hospital, though. In his first few days on the ward I saw a reflection of myself as I was at the beginning. Flat out, back-ache, unable to sleep, dry mouth, desperate for a sip of water, struggling across a vast, infinite desert of dulled pain and fatigue and the drawing up of the body's resources. His wife had brought him quite stylish pyjamas – black, green and red stripes. He looked smart, but he seemed alarmed much of the time. One night he needed a naso-gastric tube inserted to suck out the pools of bile in his stomach. The curtain was pulled round his bed, but he couldn't tolerate the tickling as the thin pipe was passed down the back of his nose. A male staff nurse was doing his best to encourage a smooth passage.

'Just swallow now, Michael.'

The sound of Michael retching cannoned round the ward. He spewed. We heard the gush as the staff nurse was hosed with bile. We started tittering.

'Just swallow. Relax. Swallow. Here it comes. One, two, three . . . '

Gush! This time with a groan of despair as the bile gurgled in his throat. The staff nurse must have been drenched again. He stayed calm.

'Now come on. We're not getting anywhere.'

Michael was gasping. 'I can't stand it. Please. Take it out.'

'I have to put it in. You know that. We're halfway there.'

I knew the feeling. It feels like a strand of half-cooked dry spaghetti is being pushed up your nostril. It touches the back of the throat and, much as dry spaghetti won't initially soften and curl into the pan of hot water, so the tube won't turn the corner easily and it jabs against the soft tissue. Gagging is spontaneous.

'OK,' said the nurse. 'Hold on for a moment. We'll stop there.' Silence. In the ward we held our breath. 'Ready? Right. Here we go again. Now, swallow.'

Instantaneously, effortlessly, Michael barked. I heard the force of his bile come up. Like a tap being turned on hard.

'Christ, I'm sorry,' he moaned. He was whimpering now. The ward was transfixed. Nurses tried to carry on as normal, but we were all quietly astonished. Twice more Michael repeated his performance before the tube was finally in place. When the curtain was eventually drawn back and the sodden nurse had retired, Michael was red-faced, sheepish, exhausted. He looked at me and shrugged. A nurse brought him some clean pyjamas. His stylish stripy ones were taken away, probably to be incinerated. Ten minutes later and he was dressed the same as me. Green poly-cotton. Stamped with a large black logo of institutionalization. 'Property Of Westminster Hospital & The Riverside Health Authority.' It had seemed like a rite of passage.

Blood-pressure readings. One hundred and twenty over sixty, one hundred over eighty. I never fully understood the differential. Nor could I ever see the thin line of mercury in the glass thermometers when they were held up to the light for temperature readings, or feel my pulse pumping in my own wrist, or make sense of the results from the thumb pricks that

79

drew blood for my blood-sugar litmus tests, but I followed all their patterns closely. Blood pressure, temperature, pulse – these are the basic observations of daily life in hospital. Once established, however, I would memorize my temperature movements and be able to quote them at the Prof to one decimal place to disarm him on ward round. After a while I could even guess my temperature quite accurately. I could feel it rising:

37.6 . . . 37.8 (learning to recognize the faint sickness it induced)
37.9 . . . 38.1 (the loss of concentration and desire to talk to anyone)
38.2 . . . 38.3 (a slight fogging of the eyes and the dry, sucking aridity in my head and the back of my neck)
38.1 . . . 37.9 (the levelling out and the dropping off)
37.7 (a severe sweat during an afternoon nap, or in the middle of a restless night, maybe a pang of hunger, a need to piss seemingly incessantly, and the final falling back to . . .)
36.9 . . . 36.8 (like some calm valley after a long ascent)

Artificially nourished and doped up with drugs, I noticed my hair start to fall out. In the mornings there would be a fine carpet of it on my pillow, and strands would be left hanging from my fingers if I ran my hand through it. I let it grow and swept it back. Audrey, Tracey's mum, said she never knew I had naturally wavy hair. She said I was very lucky. I let my beard grow too. I felt like Robinson Crusoe, and cornily imagined myself romantically tossed by fate, resolute, adaptable. Sometimes I'd ask my mother for the mirror she kept in her handbag and hold it up to my face and see a man I didn't recognize, with soft, serious eyes. It was a face of shadows and hollows, and of something learnt. When I was allowed to go to the bathroom to wash myself, I would stand in front of the mirror and look at that same face for minutes on end and would always feel strangely respectful and would quietly say, 'Keep going', impressed by the patience I saw reflected. My eyes would burn back at me.

I noticed how the weather and the outside world held no interest for me. The weather was for other people, out there in their offices and one-roomed flats, their garden sheds and their caravans, for people running for cover on the rain-spattered streets or tramping through the summer's thick, sulphurous, city air. Tracey and my mum would comment on it, even after a two-minute stroll to the pub on the corner or the nurses-home canteen – how it was mild or muggy or close or fresh. It altered their moods. Summer mornings in ITU had brought Tracey in wearing summer dresses, her bountiful eyes full of hope and light. Humid afternoons meant my mother sitting by a window tugging at the shoulders of her shirt, nurses sighing, a languorous stillness that brought a clock-stopping torpidity to the hours after lunch.

The newspaper reports lost their importance too. Corruption scandals raged, whole countries were imploding, but more often than not I closed the page, simply too listless or self-centred to pay attention. And even when the test cricket was being broadcast on my transistor radio – something I often looked forward to – I found myself drifting away into myself or I'd let the earpiece fall on to the pillow and Tracey would lean over and pick it up to put it back and I would just shrug indifference and roll my head back into the middle of the pillow, hoping for nothing more than a comfortable indentation in the polyester filling, so that I wouldn't have to move or lift my head for half an hour, and so avoid using the muscles down in my belly. I couldn't care. I couldn't care at all much of the time. About anything.

From this quiet disengagement came self-absorption, as I watched and listened out for myself. I regularly seemed to leave myself, and became ego-less, free-floating, non-doing, motionless but for my eyes flicking and blinking, like a lizard on a rock, basking in the alcohol-like fug of Voltarol or the pleasure of being temporarily released from the effects of drugs or pain, until my bed-ridden arse would ache again and I'd have to move, pinching my buttocks together, lifting my pelvis off the mattress, uncrossing my feet to find my calf muscles had gone to sleep again. And maybe another hour would have passed. I would have slumped, my back no longer cushioned in the plump pillows but cross-braced over the bed, a creaking ship's timber, my neck impacted into the top pillow like the straw in a packing-case. And if I was feeling strong I would reach up for the monkey-bar above my bed and haul myself upright until my back was straight and I was sitting on my sitting-bones, my legs stretched out in front of me like a child, my head loosed and freed, a periscope, cool air passing behind me. And in these hours, often with Tracey silently reading, I felt no anger or resentment, no festering rage at such seeming injustice, at such a seeming non-life, for the question 'Why me?' only begs the question 'Why anyone?' and the interior world I began to inhabit was not a landscape of fear and stress and acrimony but one where a recognition of my frailty and mortality fed a kind of strength. It felt stylish to be so unwell. I was important to people. To Tracey, my family, surgeons and doctors. And I felt I had the scoop on life and death and everyone else was still running around after it. And should death have come nearby again, as it did on ITU, I would have felt I had slipped under its net once, and perhaps I would do so again. Nonchalantly. With a degree of flair.

The hot sunny afternoons on the ward made me think of riding home from school in the summer. I'd often find my parents stretched out on the lawn. I'd ride my bike straight down the side of the house, past the dustbins and down to the shed at the end. The sun-loungers would be out. My dad never sunned his back but concentrated on his front. The Ambre Solaire oil would mat his chest hair until it glistened, and he'd sweat it out on hot afternoons flat on his back, all dewy with perspiration. He'd have come down in shorts, not trunks, and an unbuttoned short-sleeved pale-blue cotton shirt with Airtex panels that I liked more than his Greek-style cotton smock-shirt that pulled on over the head and had two front pockets at waist level – one for his lighter, one for his non-filter cigarettes.

He liked Turkish tobacco and was the first person I ever saw smoking Camel. One of the reasons he fell in with his old friend Brian Rix when they met for the first time in the Air Force at Scarborough was because Brian smoked Perfectos Finos and his family was sending him two hundred a week. He smoked Three Castles when I was young. Green packet. Or Gold Flake. There was a game where I had to count how many 'l's' were on the box. I always missed one.

My mum would have brought some work down to the garden in a beach-bag. Freelance magazine features – sometimes something big on Richard Burton and Liz Taylor, but often 1,200 words on Trevor Howard or Susan Hampshire or a profile on Noel Edmonds. She'd always bring me back signed photos. Roger Moore. James Galway. The Scaffold. She once asked of Noel Edmonds, 'Were there any strong musical influences in your life during your teens?' He replied, 'Absolutely none. I had no musical convictions or deep-seated knowledge. I've been lucky that my whole career has been as a disc jockey.'

They would both have just settled down when the phone would ring. I hated this moment. There would be a frantic ninety seconds while one of them would launch themselves out of their deck-chair, knocking something over, and sprint round to the front of the house, let themselves in, and race up the stairs to the first floor to catch it before it stopped ringing. There wasn't an extension at ground level, and the promise of 'a piece for *Vanity Fair*' meant the phone couldn't be ignored. Mum would sometimes have even left it on the back-bedroom window-sill so they could hear it ring early, but that meant precious time was lost in getting to it. Often it would stop ringing just as we'd hear my dad thundering into the bedroom, and then we'd listen to him cursing and shouting at it.

Friday and Saturday nights were the hospital's fight nights. There would often be a late admission on to the ward a few hours after the pubs shut and clubland got under way. A geezer would be trolleyed in out for the count with severe concussion

84

and be put into one of the spare beds freed up after the end-of-week discharges.

A thickset man was levered into one of the beds opposite me one night. He snored and farted his way through the small hours and then woke with a start as the ward ground into life again at 6.30, disorientated and still half-pissed.

A nurse came over with some warm cornflakes. 'Breakfast, love?'

'Wha . . . ?'

I don't think he could believe he had been woken. He rolled over in disgust and went back to sleep until the doctors came round at eight. They left him sleeping but made him 'Nil By Mouth' – someone had obviously punched him hard enough the night before to warrant caution – and the little plastic sign was hung over his head.

He finally came to around ten. He looked fiercely unwell. Blotchy and grim-faced, he threw back the sheets and stood up. He certainly didn't expect to find himself in a back-to-front hospital gown. He fiddled with the tassels unsteadily. All that remained of his best gear from the previous night was a pair of socks.

He stopped a nurse. 'My clothes?' It came out in a croak. He cleared his throat.

'Patients' Property,' she said, speeding past. 'You'll get them later. You can have a bath if you want. Not too hot, though.'

He fumbled with the back of the gown, tugging it over his bum-crack, and shuffled off to the bathroom.

Half an hour later he reappeared. I could see he was hungry. He sniffed round the tea-and-biscuits trolley as it went by. I could see him lining it all up in his mind – eggs, bacon, sausage, tomato, beans, fried slice, mug of tea.

He stopped another nurse. 'Any chance of something to eat? I'm starving.'

'Sorry, love.' She pointed to the sign above his bed. 'Not for now, anyway.'

'But I'm starving.'

'I'm sure, but Doctor's said – not me. It's probably for your own good.'

'But I'm starving. Cup of tea, then?'

'Sorry, love. No can do. You've taken quite a knock. I'll see if you can have sips of water after eleven.'

He sat down heavily on his bed. His face was grazed down one side, and a swelling was coming up under his left eye.

A doctor arrived. 'Ah, Mr Piper. In the land of the living at last. Glad you could join us. Now then, what can you tell us about last night, mmm?'

He hesitated. 'Erm, dunno.' He hesitated again. Nothing was coming. 'I went down Victoria. Earlyish.' He cleared his throat. 'Just a quiet drink.'

'Who brought you in?'

'Dunno.'

'It was around 1.30.'

'Dunno. Some mates, 'spect. Don't remember.' He was spectacularly dormant.

The doctor pressed on. 'Mr Piper, you were found by two police officers crawling through the flower-bed on the round-about at Lambeth Bridge with no shoes on, bleeding from a head wound. Do you have any recollection of this?'

'Maybe.'

'Maybe. I see . . . ' The doctor was looking at some notes. 'And what about your head, Mr Piper? It looks like you were hit with some kind of iron bar.'

Such grisly tales often unfolded on Sunday mornings and made something of the slow weekends.

It's five past six. The curtains have been pulled round my bed. A staff nurse and a student nurse have pulled my sheets back. My abscess has been draining into its plastic bag for several days – red, deep-red, mucous.

'Close your eyes. Relax,' they say.

I have been dreading this moment. The drain is to be pulled half out. Through the skin and flesh. I can feel them fiddling with the stitch that holds it in place. I can hear scissors.

'Breathe in after three. One, two, three . . . '

I breathe in. The plastic pipe is withdrawn. How far? An inch? A foot? And in that moment I am reeling with anxiety. I stop my mouth with the back of my own hand. I feel my teeth pressing through the skin. In my mind I see the pipe pulling free of the wound, like a shoe pulls away from fresh bubble gum. I feel the pipe moving through my flesh like a pencil through tight polystyrene. I hear the blood flooding to the site. I smell putrefaction. Illness.

A million brilliant midsummer afternoons rush through me – days on bikes, horse-racing, driving fast, pebble beaches, earthworks, hill forts, swathes of corn, disused railway lines, cold gin, open windows, sunlight turning rivers into tinsel, lollies, poppies, dog-rose. I'm scrambling up a hillside in shadow and the air is cool and my feet slip and the earth is loose and the dust is under my nails and in my hair and mouth and I grasp at small rocks and thistles that have no roots and the grit fills

my shoes, my scuffed shoes, and I have no puff and the wound in my
side is open and hot and I know I should have stayed on the track and
I want to go home and I am going to fall and the ridge is still above
me and the sun is on the ridge and a plateau of grass and wild flowers
is behind it and over it the brilliant midsummer afternoon recedes.

The staff nurse coughs. He pulls off his latex gloves. The watch on his
shirt is upside down. Time stood on its head. Is it twenty past six or ten
o'clock? The nurse says I can take my hand out of my mouth now. I have
left little red toothmarks on the surface. I suck in saliva. The sterilized
stainless-steel trolley is wheeled away silently, and the curtain is pulled
back. I look under the bedclothes. The drain looks the same as before.

When I was finally allowed to drink, I had no appetite for tea
or coffee but drank sweet soft drinks in crazes – weak Ribena
and orange barley water cooled by ice-cubes from the ice-
dispenser in the hospital kitchen. I was only allowed little 30
ml capfuls on the hour. They turned into treats. I'd watch the
second hand going round on my watch. Thirteen minutes and
twenty-one seconds to go, and then I could reach for another
capful. It was like knocking back half-measures from a non-
alcoholic pub.

Fluids were encouraged, to keep my kidneys well flushed.
Sometimes additional bags of saline would be rigged up to add
to the fluids from my dripped-feeding system, especially when
I was back to Nil By Mouth for a couple of days. I would lose
the desire to drink, and lie for hours on end, motionless, except
for having to piss. One night I woke to find the sheets and
mattress soaking wet. I thought I had wet the bed. I called the
night nurse over. The drip in my arm was throbbing, and it

was the bandage dressing around it that was wet through. The vein had closed off and the saline was welling up in the site and then dribbling out over my wrist. My arm was fat and red. The nurse pulled the line out and I went back to sleep with my arm supported above me on three pillows. If I laid it on the bed, the stinging and swollen vein kept me awake. In the morning the houseman arrived with his Velcro tourniquet to put another line in. To me, it was like jabbing the needle adaptor on a bicycle pump into the bladder of a football.

My TPN feed-bag was changed every twenty-four hours. Everything was sterilized. Gloves, tongs, bags, paper. As the valve on the bag was opened, I'd watch the fluid run round the twists and bends of the feed-pipe with the same fascination I had as a child with curly straws. The nurse would let a small amount pass out into a tray and then reconnect me. The pumps on the ward were older and less reliable than the flashier ones on ITU. Little air bubbles would get trapped in the collar of the pump, setting off the alarm. A nurse, or sometimes Tracey, would pull the thin flexible pipe free and flick it until the bubbles broke up and dispersed into the milky liquid. The pipe could then be reinserted and the pump started up again. Sometimes this went on all night.

I was gradually encouraged to start eating again. The abscess had been a bad interruption and had set me back a week or two. Nobody had much idea of what I would be able to tolerate. A patient with an 85 per cent loss of small intestine was a new experience for almost everyone, and it still wasn't clear whether the mechanics of the gut were definitely working and the passage of food was going to be unimpeded. I began again with some soup and a slice of white bread. The senior dietitian came down to see me to explain the basis of a low-residue diet – foods that put the gut under little stress, were easy to absorb, and left little waste behind. She left me with a few guidelines that I could have worked out for myself – rice, boiled potatoes, white meat, fish – and asked me to consider build-up drinks. She ran through the flavours. Tropical fruit, chocolate, lime. A future of boiled cod and lime glucose drinks stretched before me. I wasn't listening by the end. She left me and told me to pick my meals out carefully from the hospital food trolley.

For the next couple of days I tried a mouthful of cold turkey, mashed potato, tomato soup, all with little enthusiasm. The food on the ward was like old-fashioned school dinners – beef curry, lamb cutlets, boiled carrots, ham rolls, custard – and the smell that rose from the serving-dishes and warming-ovens was like hotel kitchens or cross-Channel-ferry cafeterias. Arnold opposite me would greet each course with an 'I say!' and then proceed to eat everything with an eagerness that baffled me. Custard was a big favourite with Arnold. He was dedicated. Every spoonful was appreciated.

In the mornings the shop trolley would come round. White-haired women in cardigans and tweed skirts – all volunteers – would call out 'Shop trolley!' in bright, sharp, church-hall voices. The trolley was laden with Lucozade, soft drinks, Handy Andies, chocolate, talcum powder, Rich Tea biscuits, toothpaste. Nobody bought anything. Most of us were barely on water most of the time.

★

Once a week the library trolley would come round too. Len Deighton, Agatha Christie, Dick Francis. Ghost-written biographies. Books on fishing. All in hardback, with plastic covers dulled by fingering and sunlight.

'What do you like?' the woman would say brightly. 'Detectives? Crime? Something light, or something exciting? How about something romantic?'

'Have you got anything historical?' a new man in the next bed asked.

'Ooh, I don't think so.'

'Something factual. A historian. A. J. P. Taylor perhaps.'

'Hmm, let me see,' she said, spinning the trolley round. 'What about *The Eagle Has Landed*?'

'No, never mind.'

'How about *Jaws*?'

'No, thank you.'

'I've got some sport,' she ventured.

'No. Really.' He returned to his paper.

'Golf?'

'No.'

'Kevin Keegan?'

A young German came in one evening with stomach pains. He spoke little English, but the nurses – as is the English way – would not slow down the patter of their speech or ease their grammar to help him understand. They just spoke louder.

'Now then, sir. How are you feeling in yourself?' said a staff nurse the next morning.

Awkward phrase. He looked puzzled.

The nurse spoke louder, like we do to old people, simply turning the clauses round in her sentence. 'In yourself. How are you feeling? All right, are we?'

The royal 'we'. That should fox him.

He struggled to speak. He sounded so German. 'Sorry . . . I . . . ' He opened his eyes wide and shrugged helplessly.

The nurse tried again. She put one hand down on the bed. 'Any pain?' Blank response. She sighed a little petulantly and spoke up. 'ARE YOU IN ANY PAIN?'

Three or four of us looked up at the volume of this. The German started to look round the room for help.

The nurse tried once more. 'Hurting? Anywhere?'

Still nothing.

She had started to include gestures. It was like a bad round of charades. She put both her hands to her head, placed the palms against her temples, and shook her head from side to side while saying, 'In your head? Any pain? Pain. Up here. In your head?'

I expect there would be with all that shaking.

Strangely, however, this new action seemed to stimulate meaning, and the German's eyes brightened. He said loudly, 'No. I slept well.' He was shaking his head too. For a moment the two of them looked stark staring mad, each shaking their heads, one with her hands clasped round her ears, and talking so loudly.

His girlfriend came in. When she left later he was bored and lonely, sighing loudly and turning over and over on his bed. After two days of not eating he was brought some breakfast. His girlfriend was in to see him early that day. The look on their faces when the food arrived was one of complete astonishment. The

British NHS breakfast – Rice Krispies with warm milk, two slices of untoasted white Sunblest, a pat of warm butter, a tiny plastic tub of watery fruitless jam, and coffee made with coffee powder from an industrial-size tin of Maxwell House – is perhaps a weak spot in the service. It hardly surprised me when their astonishment quickly ascended into covert derision. She started to flick Rice Krispies at him. He performed origami with the bread. He looked so much better for this. Perhaps the breakfast is intended to get people back on their feet. Shock therapy. When the doctors came round he was bright-eyed and free of pain. They discharged him. As he left he took out his wallet from the breast pocket of the candy-striped, faded, flannelette, fifties-style hospital pyjamas he had been given to wear by the Riverside Health Authority and asked a surgeon who to pay for his stay. When he learnt it had all been on the house he was thoroughly defeated and left the hospital just shaking his head in wonder and disbelief at our free and brilliant shambles.

A week after the abscess operation half my staples were removed. The wound had been oozing a little bit in the middle. A dressing change was in order. Every other staple was to be taken out; the rest a few days later. I lay flat and tipped my head up to watch. Cold sterilizing liquid was rubbed along the site, leaving the clips like a polished single-gauge railway line. I admired the surgeon's work for a moment. The clips came out quite painlessly. A small lever was pushed under each one and then used to ease out the staple. One of them pinged on to the floor. We laughed at that. The eight-inch healing scar ran down the right-hand side of my belly button. One of the nurses said I was lucky, because sometimes they go straight through it, leaving patients without a belly button at all. Fourteen clips came out. I half expected the whole thing to come apart. A fresh dressing was put on and the nurses went away.

The physios were on to me straightaway for exercise. At first I would walk with one of them over to the TV room or out into the corridor and on to the glass-covered walkway that linked the main hospital block with the Page Street block. It was a little promenade. Patients and relations would use it for a quick smoke. Somehow the glass must have given them the impression of outdoors and fresh air. It must have seemed like their cigarette smoke wouldn't be noticed, but the corridor was largely enclosed and the smoke would get trapped, leaving it slightly fuggy like a station waiting-room. Signs were regularly left to encourage smokers to go outside, and some of them would slip out on to the balcony alongside. Some people would be chatting, some grieving, others consoling. Patients in wheelchairs on their way to X-ray would pass by with porters. I'd stand and watch people park their cars in the road below. Sometimes I'd see one of my doctors on his way to lunch and have the urge to knock on the window and wave.

'Sliced you up good and proper then, didn't they?'

I am in the TV room. I have just given the other man in the room a brief description of what has happened to me. He is wearing green NHS pyjamas and a white martial-arts-style dressing-gown.

'They've cocked me up once already,' he says. He is smoking Embassy. The short filter ones.

'Oh yes?'

94

'Yeah! 'Scuse my French, but I reckon . . . ' He leans forward and lowers his voice. '. . . they're all fucking useless.'

I raise my eyebrows.

'All of them! Doctors. Surgeons. The lot. They've all got their minds on other things. All that private work. Harley Street. They're all fucking loaded.' He pulls on his Embassy.

I don't want to be drawn in. I don't want to say anything, so I open my eyes in interested disbelief.

'Take me, right. They've been in once already,' he says. He gestures to his chest. 'Missed it. Missed it! Can you fucking believe it? Mickey Mouse, I can tell you. I shouldn't be smoking, though. They don't like it. Still, you only live once.' He blows out smoke, affecting boredom, before carrying on. 'Can you eat, then?'

I shake my head and flick my eyes up to the drip food-bag I've got with me.

'I'm fucking starving. The food you get in here!' He shakes his head. 'Is your ward noisy?'

'I don't know. No, not really. It's all right.'

'I can't stand it. It's not the people in the beds; it's the nurses. Yak, yak, yak, all day long.'

I look at the TV screen. Colour images. The sound is off. A little green megaphone with a cross through it is winking in the top left-hand corner. He starts again.

'D'you watch this Channel-4 bollocks, then?'

That's it. Enough. I push myself up out of the chair. 'No, no. It's all yours.' I roll my drip-stand towards the door and over the metal-strip plate in the doorway. I have to take it at speed to get the wheels up and over. Some days it refuses, like a horse at a fence, and the wheels slam to a halt. Today it glides over and I'm away.

★

95

The day after my first set of staples came out was a Sunday. My dad popped in on his own. The ice had been broken. He was open and relaxed. He opened his carrier bag and got out a box. He'd been into Oxford specially. He unwrapped the tissue paper and got out the shoes. We admired them greatly, looking at them from all angles. And then he pulled up the bedclothes and put them on my dry, bare feet. I waved them around and kept them on for twenty minutes. He touched my feet gently. I felt his hands on my skin. It felt strange. I realized the only contact we'd had for years was shaking hands.

He used to come home late from Soho clubs, often with two or three friends, when I was very young. I'd hear them come crashing in. They would sit up drinking into the small hours, playing cards and listening to records – Bud Powell, Roland Kirk, Charlie Parker. He brought a couple of musician friends back one night and then came to my room. It was dark. I saw his figure against the landing light. I heard laughter downstairs. The tip of his cigarette was glowing. He lifted me out of the bed. I must have been young. I felt the crisp wool of his suit rough up against my skin, the cigarette packet through his pocket. He carried me downstairs into the sitting-room and sat me down on the carpet in front of the hi-fi speaker. I was still half asleep. The speaker was three feet tall, part of a monophonic sound system, with a brass grill across it. When it wasn't on, I used to run my hand down its smooth polished sides. It seemed so huge and solid, like the front of an enormous car. I'd hang my Action Men from it, fitting their rubber fingers into the holes and imagined them rock-climbing on a sheer face. My dad settled down with his friends again.

The music throbbed over me, warm music, rich in tone, until I fell asleep curled up on the floor.

His first break came with the Carl Barriteau band during the war. Barriteau was from Trinidad. His band was *it*. Number two in the *Melody Maker* poll that year. My dad was thrilled. He had volunteered for the Air Force after leaving school in Glasgow but had been given an eighteen-month deferral because he was only seventeen. He met a pianist called McCormack who was homesick for Glasgow and simply offered to exchange his job playing for Barriteau for my dad's gig with the Jack Chapman band at the Albert Ballroom. My dad jumped at the chance.

One night, after playing in Leamington Spa, he happened to call home. It was 1944, two years since volunteering. He was shocked to learn that his call-up papers had been there for two weeks. The next morning he called Reading and cheekily asked for an extension, saying he was on tour. He was told flatly to report as ordered. He stalled for a day, but at lunch a car drove up and two corporals got out ready to drag him away. He promised to report to Scarborough by ten the next morning and he got away with it.

He got to Scarborough on time. At the call-up he was wearing a pin-stripe suit and Tommy Dorsey glasses with clear glass in, just for effect. A huge corporal was shouting.

'Anyone 'ere called Watt?'

My dad stepped up. 'I've been on tour with Carl Barriteau.'

'Carl Barriteau! Let me carry your suitcase.'

He was taken to the induction centre at the Adelphi Hotel, where an officer grilled him.

'Now, look here, Watt. Explain your absence.'

'Sorry sir. I did volunteer, sir, but it's been nearly two years and I was on tour with Carl Barriteau. I play decent piano though.'

He was let off jankers and after the interview, just to cap it off, the officer invited him to the officers' mess 'to have a practice'.

In the evening, after he'd gone, I was waiting for a new feeding-system bag to come up. My abscess drain was gone, I had no naso-gastric tube and, after another swelling in my arm, my fluid drip had been temporarily removed. For the first time in weeks I was disconnected from the hospital. I asked suddenly if Tracey could wheel me outside for a push-about. The nurses said OK, and one of them capped off the line in my chest. I started to get dressed. I wanted to wear real clothes for an hour. My trousers were enormous, and my jacket hung on my shoulders as if over a wire coat-hanger. I was still hunched over. I had Tracey put my new shoes from my dad on my feet, and a nurse fetched us a wheelchair. We went down in the lift and out through reception.

The air outside was evening air – settled on the city, day-old. We passed by the news-stand on the corner, crossed over, and passed along a covered wooden pavement made by a construction company for the building site opposite the hospital. The cars were noisy. Breezes blew. They disturbed me, flicking at my hair, whipping out from the side-streets. An insect landed on my jacket. I flicked it off. A dog barked. It startled me. We crossed over again by the roundabout at

Lambeth Bridge and Tracey pushed me into the garden that runs from the bridge up to Westminster. We trundled under trees. I felt tiny, empty, perplexed. Wind off the river rustled the huge canopy of leaves above me. It was loud. I couldn't speak. The trunks and branches were big and strong, sap-full and lean. The river's embankment was black and brick. We stopped. Cut into the wall were two steps up and a viewing platform. Tracey pulled me up out of the chair and hugged me. She was tearful. We stood there for minutes, the wind still in the trees, loud and restless, and I stood there limp on her shoulder and I thought how the line of trees was like a tunnel stretching ahead and behind and we were alone and halfway along it.

A few tourists passed. We climbed up to look at the river. I was transfixed by the water. Thick, muscular currents swirled below me. There was so much life in it. By the wall, little eddies rippled on the surface. Waves slapped against the dark stone. I wanted to fall in and be held up, borne afloat, rushed downstream in turning circles of disorientation, under bridges, past children waving and tugs and river boats, police launches and dredgers, and down through the suburbs and the playing-fields and boat clubs to some wide delta with meadows and plains and green hills behind and the shimmering sea, salt flats and seabirds and air so fresh it would tear at my lungs, rich in oxygen and dewiness. Tracey asked if I was cold. I shivered a little. We climbed down and I got back in the chair and we headed back.

FIVE

Tracey stayed until gone nine that night. The ward was quiet in the evening. She got on to my bed and sat on top of the bedclothes to read, while I lay on my side with my head on her lap. The nurses didn't mind. Lying on my side was a new treat after weeks on my back. It was so special. The smell of her near me. The feeling of warmth on my face.

There is a photograph of the pinboard in the flat we shared after we first met at university in Hull in late 1981. Vote Labour, June 9th. Robert Doisneau's kiss. The cover from the second Smiths single. Arthur Miller. A box of Swan Vestas. The cover of *Paris Blues* ('The stinging novel of a man seeking escape in a world of cellar clubs, drugs and hot jazz'). Eddie Cochrane. A flyer for Tony Marchant's *Welcome Home*. Vivien Goldman. A paying-in slip. A photo of the Humber bridge and a Hull–Brough–Goole–London InterCity timetable. A phone bill. A Women in Literature reading-list. A sewing-kit. A Yale key.

Is this who we were? Or who we wanted to be at least? I see us as always having been the same. We will always be nineteen. I will always be Tannoying her in the Union building on the first day, saying, 'If Tracey of The Marine Girls is in the building, could she please come to Reception now.' And she will always be appearing in red scuffed stilettoes, and I will always be saying, by way of introduction, 'We share the same record label. Have you brought your guitar?' We were teenagers in bands, and for that reason found ourselves bound together as much by what we were against as by what we had in common. We seemed instantly close, although we came from very different families. She seemed unpretentious and unfamiliar to me, not like the boisterous girls I had grown up around back home.

In the top left-hand corner is a picture of us taken by one of my lecturers (a part-time photographer) during an afternoon that produced the first publicity shot for the band we formed. Me – 501s, white socks, black suede creepers, chunky black sweater, corduroy cap. Tracey – abstract-print fifties skirt, white socks, black pointed slip-ons, grey sweatshirt with the sleeves cut off, Alice band. She is looking down. I am looking at the camera. The surroundings are incongruous, and probably explain why we never used the picture. We are the post-punk generation and we are sitting cross-legged on my lecturer's Indian bean-bag with a cheese plant and a Victorian rocking-horse in the background. We look sulky and intense – not surprising under the circumstances.

I went round to Tracey's house one morning before we'd started going out with each other and found her sleeping in the scarf I had matter-of-factly lent her the night before. People say we have always been formidable. It's not how it seems from the inside.

It's three in the morning and I am lying in bed watching one of the night-time agency nurses eating chocolates one after the other. She is leafing through a two-day-old copy of the Daily Mirror and wearing a cardigan. I am wearing earplugs, yellow foam earplugs. They muffle sound and amplify the inside of my head. I can hear the fluids in my ears and sinus cavities. When I lie still there is a continuous sound, like waves booming in underground caves or jet engines heard from the cabin on a long-haul flight. When I twist my head my hair moves against the pillow. It is loud, like the close-up heavy breath of a sleeping man. I close my eyes again and drift and I am in an under-sea world. Chocolates float dreamily past. I doze for a few minutes.

I open my eyes and the lights are on around the bed in the corner. That's Victor's bed. The curtains are drawn. Victor is Hungarian, I think. He speaks little English. I see shadows of nurses. He has had bad trouble with his kidneys. He pees blood a lot. He has thick white hair, swept back like Anton Walbrook. His wife comes after work. All they seem to do is argue. She is small, like a bird – a hawk – with short Samuel Beckett hair and a face weathered and tanned and creased. She wears trousers, and despairs with the expansive silent-movie gestures of sorrow and anguish, so demonstrative and out of place in an English hospital. He rolls his head away and ignores her. He is very unhappy. When I catch another patient's eye he winks. When I catch Victor's eye he shrugs. His mouth is turned down. He can't get comfy in his bed. He sighs a lot. He has learnt the word for coffee and how to turn down milk and sugar, although he grimaces when he drinks the powdered stuff he is given. I think of how thick and strong the coffee probably is in Budapest, served in dark cafés with wooden bars, ornate and cosmopolitan like the art-nouveau entrance halls of Berlin.

I doze again. My earplug aqualung is noisy. Hungarian chocolates sparkle on the seabed amid discarded chandeliers and marble. Anton Walbrook swims below me.

I open my eyes again. It is 5.15. Two hours have passed. Two hours' unbroken sleep. I can't believe my luck. Victor is asleep now, and the nurses have gone. Tim is sitting up with his reading-light on. He has an Indian wife and a beautiful daughter. They all seem very close. They come and see him in the afternoons. They wear saris. When he gets up to pad around, Tim wears an Indian cotton skirt and an old woolly cardigan. He reads books, and sometimes comes over with an idea for Tracey's crossword. He is a doctor himself, but he has barely heard of my illness. He wears half-rimmed glasses to read, and scratches his beard a lot. It makes quite a noise. I always look up when he scratches his beard. I wish he were in the bed next to me. We could have the odd chat. I nod off again. I have been sitting up all night. I can't lie down or twist since the abscess operation.

I dream I am in Bombay now. I am riding on an elephant. There is gunfire, and there are people running towards me. Someone is tugging at my arm, trying to pull me off. I resist. The tugging won't stop. I open my eyes. Sarah, kind Sarah, a nurse who always works nights, is trying to get my arm out from under the bedclothes to get at my drip without waking me. I smile. She says something. I see her lips move. I pull out one of my earplugs. It is 6.30. Drug round. Temperature. Blood pressure. Pulse. Breakfast soon. Maybe I could try some cornflakes today. Wouldn't be too demanding.

The man in the cubicle next to me died the next day. He would cough in the night. Weak, tight coughs, like the light puttering of a single-engined plane. In his last few days he called out for the nurses, his quietly desperate voice struggling to be heard over the bustling morning activity. And when they went to him all he asked for was for a curtain to be left open or a light to be turned off. His daughter would come and see him, always bringing someone else with her. They'd have come on the bus, after work – a long, arduous journey across the city. As father and daughter, they would never really talk to each other. He was too ill, and she was too long-sufferingly maternal and overworked to be relaxed. 'Sit up, Dad.' 'Don't play with it, Dad!' 'More oxygen, Dad?' – delivered as reprimands born from too much caring.

I never asked what was wrong, but everyone seemed to know there was nothing that could be done. He seemed resigned, ready for the end. His daughter brought him clean pyjamas every other day. I must have been out for a short walkabout or something on the day he died, because when I came back he wasn't there any more. The cubicle was empty and his bed had been remade. The curtains were drawn back, and a cleaner was mopping the floor.

By the evening a new patient was installed – a man with a smart moustache, blue ironed pyjamas, leather slippers and a drip in his neck. He was calling on nurses to see if he was allowed to drink.

'Would it be bad form of me to ask for a sip of water? Don't want to muck things up.'

His accent was crisp, like an old-fashioned fighter pilot's. He seemed keen to get off on the right foot with everyone – keen to please, ready to obey, as though he were in a prep-school sickbay and the nurses were all Matron. 'No trouble. Just say the word. Don't suppose we could pop the window open?' He tried out some chatty banter with the surgical team – 'Expect you'll want a peep under the old bonnet?' – but they were typically dry and measured in response. His posh voice sailed over the cubicle wall. Wry smiles were exchanged between the two men in the beds opposite me. A couple of winks.

That night I was kept awake by the sheer absence of coughing.

From the bog window on the ward I can see offices. I can see office workers. They don't know I'm in here. With diarrhoea. And hard pink bog paper. Pink crêpe-paper bog roll. NHS special issue. I come in here every day with diarrhoea and the hard pink crêpe paper that makes my arse sore, and they don't know. They don't know the smell of other arses and this warm seat, and the little silver pedal bin, and the little door in the wall that says 'Engineers Only'. My days are on hold. Their days are the same as they always were. They don't know what they're missing. In their offices. With things to do. Memos to write. Sandwiches to eat.

I am having a bath now. The water is hot. The nurse said, 'Not too hot.' I have been sitting in this deep old bath for fifteen minutes, the water lapping over my metal stitches. The skin around the stitches is tight and slightly puckered. My arm is over the side and my chest is half upright, to keep the drips and lines dry. The vertebrae at the base of my spine stand out like little drumlins on my back. They knock and grind on the bottom. I feel very thin today.

I have stood up now. I feel light-headed. Maybe the water was too hot. I am sitting on the edge of the bath. My toes are white and crinkly. My nails are blanched like white coral. I crouch awkwardly over the edge of the bath and wash my own hair one-handed with a plastic jug. I pull the plug out and watch the water drain away, leaving a fine mat of my hair on the chipped enamel. It comes out all the time. It bothers me. I dry my hair. The towel is covered in hair. I run my hand through my hair and my hand is covered in hair. I comb it back and the comb is full of hair. I have clean pyjamas — not that they are matching jacket and trousers, but that doesn't matter. Green top, striped bottoms. I like the ones with the drawstring waistband best. They are gentler on my stitches. I cover my armpits and balls in talc. Lovely. I brush my teeth. I haven't brushed them for a week. I am exhausted.

I have on the clean pyjamas now. I am sitting out in a chair beside my bed for the first time in a few days. My knees are bent, to be gentle on my belly, and my feet are on the edge of the bed. I have a copy of the morning paper that I paid for this morning — Tracey leaves me a little change each night before she goes, in case I want to ring her from the pay phone on wheels — and a glass of weak orange barley water on the table next to me. In my hand is a book. I am on page 12. I know Tracey will be here in a minute. She will be so happy to see me out in the chair. And I've had a bath too. She won't believe it. I'll probably need a little sleep later to make up for it. I'll keep my head in my book, wear my reading-glasses that I don't really need, and look studious and interesting for when she arrives. I have no pain this morning. Here she comes. Doesn't she walk well?

She has always walked that way. I used to watch her come home across the campus in Hull in calf-length jeans and summer shoes with bare feet even in midwinter, picking her way across the icy paving like a wader. I used to think how I never imagined I'd ever be lucky enough to have a tall, thin girlfriend. She'd wear her worn-down high heels if we went out into town in the evenings to the Cecil or the ABC for a film, or Desolation Row for drinking and dancing, and she'd clack along beside me like a real girlfriend.

When we moved in together in Hull I wrote to tell my mum. She wrote to me regularly. She wrote back very understatedly with a genuine liberal spirit, wishing us happiness, but at the bottom she'd added a typical PS – 'Just written 1,750 words on Arthur Lowe for *TV Times* for first week in July and received my ticket for my holiday in Pyrenees. Do you want anything? Aftershave? Espadrilles?! WALLET? GOLD CHAIN?! Glorious day. Garden gorgeous.'

All her letters were generally racy streams of thought and full of news. '*Dear*,' one began, '*Grandma has GONE. (No comment) We are trying to persuade her to rent a· COLOUR TV. Skipper has cemented round our garden shed in an ANTI-RAT campaign. I got a story in Nigel Dempster's column on Wednesday.*'

I came back from the TV room one afternoon to see a man the size of a house being winched down on to a special bed next to mine. It was like watching a grand piano being moved. The bed was hydraulically powered, like a dustcart. Broad, almost a double, it folded across the middle and could sit the occupant up or lay them down mechanically. Frank, the bed's occupant, was so gigantic that if he lay down he would never have got up again on his own. He was massive, like the combined halves of a heavyweight-wrestling tag team. I never really found out what he was in for, but people said he was having his stomach stapled together and his teeth wired to lose weight. They said he had been known to eat three sliced loaves (thick cut) at one sitting but was now facing a liquid diet of soups and juices fed through a straw. He was bearded and wore a white shirt that could have served as a sight-screen. I found myself just looking at him all the time. I would lie back in the very middle of my bed and watch him sleeping. When he dozed, the slow, steady stream of air that passed through his nostrils sounded deep and hollow like ventilator shafts. The bristles would flutter on his top lip, and he'd puff out air from time to time as though he were dismissing something out of hand in his sleep. His cheeks would flap like udders, and his stomach rose and fell so far that sometimes the sheets were lifted clean off the bed. He was a real-life sleeping giant.

His family came in to see him. They were huge too – big people with jowly faces and XXL T-shirts, all in cushion-soled shoes and elasticated waistbands, all drinking, eating and talking seemingly simultaneously, gathered round his bed like creatures at a watering-hole. Things looked so small in their hands. Beakers became eggcups. Newspapers were just little paperbacks. Even the children were colossal. Colossal youth. Fleshy, sugar-enriched hulks of teen and pre-teen self-consciousness.

During visitors' hours, usually in the afternoons, all sorts of relatives would set up shop by the beds, some making themselves comfy straightaway, pulling up chairs, pouring themselves a glass of squash, getting the cups of tea in, others remaining discontentedly nervous, leaning in from the edge of their seats, keeping their coats on.

Kevin's parents always brought more fruit and more fizzy drinks. Sweets too, like wine gums and Mintolas. I strained with jealousy sometimes, so bored was I with 30 ml capfuls of water. Kevin would slosh back a Tango and a handful of seedless grapes. It seemed so spoilt and Roman. He'd meticulously line the drinks up on his bedside table in descending height – barley water, blackcurrant cordial, Tango and Citrus Spring together, and maybe a mini-carton of Just Juice, and then manically roll the round fruits back and forth, back and forth, across his invalid-table under the palm of his hand while his parents watched in silence.

Bert's wife would knit, knit, knit – barely speaking to her husband – just the pickety-pick of needles and wool. She brought him library books on war and *Flypast* magazine. She kept a copy of *Cat World* in her bag. She seemed at ease. She would often turn her chair away from Bert entirely, to face the ward to keep up with the afternoon's action while Bert dozed or flicked through his mag. Sometimes she'd turn her head over her shoulder to speak to him –

'All right, love? Need a nurse?'

'No, I'm all right.'

'Cup of tea to flush you through?'

The incessant knitting would sometimes get to Bert. He'd loll his head towards her across his pillow. 'Could you stop that, love?'

'What's that?'

Pickety-pick pick pick.

'The knitting, love. Could you just stop for a bit?'

'Sorry, love. Can't hear you. I'll stop knitting.' Silence. 'Now then, what were you saying?'

Pickety-pick pick pick.

An old friend came to see me. He looked shocked as he came round the corner. I have known him since I was about five or six. He used to live in my road. He brought me books to read.

Loads of books. He thought I must be bored witless, not knowing – how could he? – that the middle distance and the inside of my own head were more interesting than books. He left them on my bedside table. Hardbacks. Stoppard. Pinter. Drama criticism. Bellow. Books we used to talk about at school twelve years ago. He kissed me on the forehead. None of my other friends do that.

When we meet, he always hugs me. I feel his bristly chin against my face. I often miss the moment, don't get my arms out in time, and he just bear-hugs me, pinning my arms to my sides. I sometimes catch my own reflection in a mirror and feel a prat. I used to think he was a hard man, but he is a very soft man.

He talked and talked. I can't remember what he said. I remember his grey jacket with its wide shoulders, though, and his bristly chin and the books, but not a word of what he said. No, that's not true. I remember one thing he said. He said he liked my beard. 'Very casual and relaxed,' he said. He sat on the bed. Really quite close to me. Other friends and family tended to sit at a distance. In a chair. But he sat close. He seemed moved. I wasn't young any more. Not a boy. We used to pretend we were brothers at school. In the playground. Marching round, arms over each other's shoulders, chanting 'Who wants to play football?' in loud, squeaky, rhythmic voices until a whole gang of us had joined up, all arms over shoulders, all chanting, wheeling round like the wings of a huge bird. When I was young I got up from the table round at his house and ran all the way home because his mother had put a plate of spaghetti bolognese in front of me. I'd seen spaghetti bolognese before, but had never been expected to eat it.

He looked at me with soft eyes. I was older now. Thinner. I tried to be natural and smiled as much as I could.

I never really expected anyone to come. I was always surprised when Tracey said a friend would be along the next day. I felt I must be uninteresting to anyone but myself, and that the sooner I sorted everything out myself and got back to how things used to be the better for everyone. My illness struck me as just a nuisance in many ways, nothing too serious, even when I was aware I was on a ventilator, or on the way up to theatre for the third time in a week, or groggy and lost in the recovery room. I thought a few more days, a quick shower and I would be right as rain. And when I wasn't fighting back I was strangely calm and resigned. I felt if someone had come up to me and said, 'I think it's time to make your will. There is only one drug left we haven't tried,' I would have just shrugged and thought, 'Never mind. Death's not such a bad prospect, all things considered. What's everyone making such a fuss about?'

Eileen, our manager at the time, visited a few times, often with her business partner, John. Eileen had dropped everything and come straight to the hospital when I was first admitted. They had had to be the ones who phoned round and cancelled our summer tour in America, and then I'm sure spent long afternoons sitting opposite each other in their tiny office in Notting Hill asking each other if I'd ever play again, or be able to record, or travel or eat or drink, feeling desperately involved but excluded too. They both came when I was first on ITU.

They seemed ill at ease. They brought me little presents. John had been out to Tandy and bought a minicomputer tennis game that ran on a battery. I tried it out a couple of times but I couldn't work out what was going on. I thought I was still knocking up when the screen flashed up that I'd just lost in straight sets. The screen was really low-resolution and I had to squint. It was exhausting. Five minutes and I was finished. Eileen brought me a copy of *Viz*. I didn't dare look at it for fear of laughing and hurting myself. For a while it lived up on the top shelf next to my bed in ITU. I used to look up at its green cover and think about asking one of the nurses to get it down so I could have a peep at one or two of the cartoons, but Johnny Fartpants and Buster Gonads didn't seem quite appropriate after four small-bowel operations and a room full of people on life-support machines. Once Eileen came on a Sunday and was a different person. She had on denim and a white roll-neck sweater. She sat by the bed. She was much more relaxed and just chatted, letting the afternoon spread out before us all, as though Sunday was a window that looked away from all concerns.

In many ways, that was how I wanted visitors to be. The most rewarding visits were when people came and didn't feel they had only half an hour in which to sympathize, adhere to an imagined code of conduct and then get out. I wanted people to stay if I had to have a short test done, wait outside if they felt happier, but then come back and stay a little longer and try to see it as normal and that I was the same. But hospital unnerves people, in the same way that being in the presence of disabled people and old, infirm people unnerves people. The proximity of death and pain is unsettling and embarrassing. The parameters of the appropriate response seem to change, and I watched friends stumbling over their self-consciousness and battling with over- or under-reaction. If I held out a hand I'd see them choking back a tear. If I were quiet for a few minutes they would feel they had overstayed their welcome. If I smiled weakly I'd feel I had inadvertently created a moment of unbearable poignancy. And curiously, because of this, I felt a huge amount of power over them. I realized I could manipulate their emotions, and I was fascinated at their impressionability. It seemed easy to exploit their good intentions and, if I chose, to turn a cough into a dying breath, a goodbye into a last farewell. Their hearts were open books, their eyes wells of sympathy. I surprised myself at the times I contemplated such duplicity – not so cruel as to ever really put it into practice, but cruel enough to consider it.

I didn't see much of my half-brothers. They each came a couple of times, but their visits were muted and awkward. I felt the family was being driven into itself by my experience. It is said a crisis can pull a family together, but strangely I thought we were forced apart and I found myself thinking how different we all were, relations as if only by chance, each wrapped up in very different versions of what was happening.

When I think of us all together I see the old family house. We had the top two floors of an Edwardian house in South London, with my grandmother living on the ground floor. After my grandmother died, my mum and dad rented out the lower flat for a while, but in the end the whole lot was sold.

I grew up and lived there until I went to university. Whenever I fly home I look out for it on clear days, banking out of the holding pattern above Heathrow, a figure of eight over Lego London. The south-west suburbs. Richmond Park. The reservoirs. Hammersmith Bridge.

I always see Christmas. We all ate turkey in the sitting-room. Every available table in the flat was put in the middle of the room and covered in red crêpe paper and then surrounded by all the available chairs. Even deck-chairs were fetched from the shed. My grandmother was summoned from downstairs and then, shortly after four o'clock, we all began. Tinsel hung from the huge gilt mirror on the wall. We were all reflected in it. The room seemed packed with people and paper and presents. At the end of lunch one year, my mum, wearing a scarlet and white floppy hat, presented my grandmother with her present from the family. It was a huge cardboard banana box of tinned food. She wouldn't keep a fridge, and food was always going off in her flat.

After we'd all watched Morcambe and Wise, my dad slipped away and started playing the piano – 'Love is Here to Stay' and 'We'll be Together Again'. He always did this. They were the songs he played to my mum when they first met when he had his band at Quaglino's. The piano was kept in my mum and dad's bedroom. There wasn't really anywhere else to keep it. Gradually the family drifted in one by one to listen and sing along quietly. Great-aunt Margery, who taught English in a school in Willesden, was allowed to perform an English pastoral, and my mum sang 'A Nightingale Sang in Berkeley Square'. Then my dad got back on the stool and hammered out some boogie-woogie with joky lyrics sung by my eldest half-brother, Simon, before climaxing with some loud ragtime to which Helen, my mum's first husband's partner, vigorously danced the charleston. We all clapped along and whistled and cheered at this. Nothing could follow Helen's routine. She often did it. It was her moment, and for several years it was the crowning moment of Christmas. After that the crowd dispersed, leaving Simon playing his own sad compositions in the style of Roy Harper. My half-sister Jennie stayed and listened for a little bit, and my mum, and then the room was empty.

I didn't like it when they put someone old and obviously ill in the bed next to me. Tracey said most of the time no one looked more haggard than me and Kevin, but, even so, I always preferred it if I got someone straightforwardly middle-aged and evidently on the mend. If they were too young – and by that I mean my age or younger – it made me think too self-pityingly about myself for my own good, and I would dwell silently and darkly for too long at a time. Too old and I immediately felt uneasy and I constantly seemed to be waiting for them to die or convulse or something. Middle-aged, though, and I felt OK. But they put Pat in next to me all the same.

Pat was yellow. An oily yellow. He was loud and old. He barked at the nurses, especially the younger ones, which made me jump.

'Bleeaarrgghh!!' he seemed to say to them.

He sat in his bed with long, lank, ratty grey hair, unshaven, in piss-stained long johns for two days before he was given clean pyjamas that he didn't want. He had wild eyes like he'd just seen something bad and it was still in front of him. He had long uncut toenails, perfectly shaped. They were filthy and as sharp as winkle-pickers, and the tips were starting to curl back under his feet. Until he spoke in sentences made up of more than two or three words, I couldn't place him at all – rich, poor, posh, ordinary. He used to detach the bag from his drip-stand when he got up to slouch off for a piss – he wasn't meant to do this – and then worsen things by holding the bag too low so the blood from his arm would flow down and back up the tube, mixing with the saline halfway, turning the fluids pink like diluted grenadine. It was a gruesome sight. The nurses told him not to, but he would forget the next time he got up and he had to have his line changed in his arm three times in the first two days because of it.

He went up to theatre a couple of days later and came back looking worse. Still jaundiced, his skin had turned more sulphurous. The days passed and he didn't look any better. His eyes were duller, and he got quieter and lay stiller. He had been given a catheter up in theatre, and he didn't try and get up so often.

He would perk up in the mornings, though, when the papers came round. Every day he asked for the *Sporting Life*. Of course the paper trolley never had it. He'd try asking for the *Racing Post*, which was even more unlikely, and then settle for the *Daily Express* and would pore over the racing pages on and off all morning. He asked one of the nurses to place bets for him a couple of times.

'It's a Carson double. Can't fail,' he barked.

We all laughed.

'Sorry, Pat,' she said. 'I wouldn't know where to start. Anyway, you don't want to be throwing your money away now, do you?'

'Look, love. It's a Cecil horse in the first and a Group winner in the second. Carson's on top. Take the money.'

She said no, but then when later in the week a winner and a dual forecast came up trumps on consecutive days, and he started bragging and complaining, one or two of us started to take him seriously and she soft-heartedly took his money for an each-way double at Kempton, and promised to go down to the bookie's at lunch-time.

The next day when the paper trolley came round we all got papers and I could sense everyone turning to the racing results first and none of us could believe it when we saw the horses had come in. Pat was crowing and coughing, laughing and spitting, fetching up huge globules of phlegm off his chest in his excitement – which was more than the physios had managed to do in a week.

'Told you. Told you. Pillar to post. Pillar to post.'

We all waited expectantly for the nurse to arrive for the late shift. At three she waltzed in grinning with the winnings. She was thrilled for him. She said she'd never been in a betting-shop before, and then told him she'd been given a tip for the St Leger if he needed one.

The girl from the hospital radio came round that evening. She had a pad of paper and was asking patients for requests. They were going to be broadcasting at 8.30, and we were to tune in on our little headsets above our beds. She seemed relaxed, wearing faded Lee jeans and a green sweater. She looked like she'd prefer to play some loud rock 'n' roll. From the beds on the other side of the ward I heard the requests.

'Tony Bennett.'

'Sinatra.'

'Anything lovely by Pavarotti.'

'What, love? A tea with two sugars, please, if you're making it.'

Somebody asked what else would be on the programme. We were told there would be something from *Cats* and that there had been quite a push for Glen Miller from Erskine Ward. I was banking on Kevin to ask for something frenzied and punky – a little New York Dolls or maybe some Stiff Little Fingers – but he was asleep. Victor didn't understand what was going on, which left me. I toyed with asking for something obscure and specific and meaningless, like 'Mouldy Old Dough' by Lieutenant Pigeon, but I hadn't the courage.

It is the day arranged for my second shot of cyclophosphamide, and Ignatius, a young Spanish student doctor, has been chosen to inject it. My eosinophil count has been creeping up, again signalling continued dangerous over-activity from my immune system. They warned me it might happen. Another chemical hammering should beat it into submission. Nobody has exactly been looking forward to it, though. Ignatius is nervous. The drug is serious. Pharmacy won't release it without special authority. Two or three consent forms have already been signed by leading doctors. Cyclophosphamide is a cytotoxic drug. Cytotoxic means cell-damaging. It was originally developed to kill malignant cells in cancer treatment, in the hope that they would be more sensitive to it than ordinary cells. In practice it has proved to be highly effective on the white cells connected with immune response, but it has to be carefully measured and monitored as it has the potential to stop all natural cell development in the bone marrow. When used a lot, cyclophosphamide can cause sterility, make hair fall out, and bring on vomiting and nausea by damaging cells in the stomach lining. Ignatius basically has his hands on a small chemical weapon.

A drip has been rigged up above me with fast-running saline. The drug has to be injected into this river as it enters my arm, to disperse quickly. Neat cyclophosphamide can cause renal failure. The drug is all contained in one needle, but must be injected laboriously over ten minutes with no gaps. It is important it goes to plan. The drip will then stay running all night, filling my system with litre upon litre of water, after which I am expected to pee every twenty minutes for the next day and a half to help flush out the drug's residue.

Ignatius takes off his watch and lays it on the bed to read the second hand going round. Steel interlinked strap. He has brown, muscular arms. He slips his thumb into the butt of the needle. He has the shakes. He tells me he has always had them but is adamant about becoming a surgeon. I smile and try to remain casual.

The drip is turned up full and he slips the needle into the line and starts to depress the plunger. Tracey is there, and Paul, the houseman. We are all quiet and watch. Paul says a few light-hearted words, and then falls quiet again. I try to relax. Ignatius is sweating. His temples are moving. He stops for a moment and flexes his hand. He has got cramp. Four minutes have passed. I close my eyes. The seriousness of the occasion sets my mind racing. I feel the cool water running in my arm.

Time stretches. I see fells and damp heather and mountain streams, hilltop tarns, Lakeland, baby waterfalls, hydroelectric power stations, fine drizzle, sheep with their fleeces stained red with dye, the reedy turf covered in droppings, scarred and striated valleys, buttresses of rock truncated and shattered into a million bits of scree, and, further down, stepping-stones, stone walls, stone bridges, dappled light, a river so clear and cold I can see boulders on the river-bed, and I want to bend down and cup my hands and drink the fresh water as it flows over my wrists. I see Rydal Water and Windermere and Tracey at the plastic wheel of a tourists motor boat, her hand in her mouth, looking all around her and across the wide water, convinced we will capsize if we are not careful and vigilant. And I see myself as a boy crossing a charred and burning stubble field towards a beach, my dad in front, my mum behind. My mum wears a turquoise towelling dress. Suddenly a lark bolts from the earth at my feet and screams into the sky above my head, singing and singing, a kite in a high wind, and my mum stops and cups her hand across her brow to see it against the bright September light and we all stop in the smouldering field and listen. I can smell the sea coming. And the dead corn. I ask my dad why the field is burning, and he says it is to enrich the soil for next year and that destruction can be for good as well as bad.

I open my eyes. Paul has gone. Ignatius has finished. He is tidying up. He slips his watch back on and clicks the strap, and then says goodbye. I say thanks, and then look round the ward. Kevin is drinking Coke and pulling at some fruit. Victor pads past forlornly in his pyjamas on his way for a crap.

I think of cyclophosphamide in my body – a wrecker, a healer, tampering, meddling with the roots of life, like an insecticide washed off fields of crops into the gullies and brooks, bubbling and frothing up like detergent, running into my veins as into rivers, and down through the topsoil and sandy loam, through underground channels and soft, *porous rocks like body tissue, to settle at the water-table which feeds my roots. And all I can think is, If and when I recover from all this, in the years ahead, will I be as I remember myself, unbowed, organic and strong? Or will I always be a weak strain, in need of shelter, susceptible to the wind and the rain?*

It is said to be quite common for patients to lose their voices temporarily if they have been on a respirator for a time. The throat can become sore, but corrects itself within a couple of days. When, after a week on ITU, I was still croaking and whispering, doctors had started taking note. They encouraged me to try to project, which was pointless, as I was trying. Tracey told me recently that they had told her at the time that my loss of voice was psychosomatic and she was to try to get me to speak. It was a sign that I was hiding in my own illness. It shocked many who came to see me. Not only did I look like Howard Hughes, but I sounded like I was about to pop off at any moment. Richard and Michelle, friends, rang the unit from their holiday in France one morning and the nurses brought the phone over. I didn't usually take calls, but I was light-headed on drugs and asked for the receiver. I whispered away in a mild haze for a few minutes. Michelle later told me how upsetting it had been.

After three weeks on St Mark's and six weeks after my first operation I was finally refezred to a throat specialist in the hospital. Things were no better. I was still croaking and rasping. He was holding an out-patients' clinic on the ground floor. Tracey helped gather up my drips and stands and I was sat in a wheelchair with my notes on my lap. The file was enormous.

Down at the clinic, it was throbbing with life. I was taken to the front of the queue. People looked at me cautiously. I felt I frightened them. Although we were all in a hospital, I looked too ill. Children were silenced by my presence. Women whispered to their husbands as I passed.

The consultant sprayed the inside of my throat with a local anaesthetic and pushed my tongue down with a wooden spatula, shaped like a large lolly-stick. Two minutes later he told me flatly one of my vocal chords was paralysed. I paused for a moment. I was stunned. I saw the end of my current life as a singer and the beginning of something even newer than I had been preparing for. I stared at the floor blankly. My voice. It frightened me more than anything else that had happened over the past weeks.

I asked him how it had happened. He said the cause was unknown, but it had probably come on as a result of heavy physical stress and suffering. He said he'd also been given to understand that neuropathy was a symptom of my illness. I asked him how long it would last.

'Difficult to say,' he said. 'A month, maybe nine months, maybe more – who knows? Depends on how badly the nerve is burnt out. Steroids might help.' He was guessing. I sat there for a moment. I told him I was a singer. He sympathized. There was a silence. He wrote his name in blue ink with a fountain pen on to a piece of paper. All consultants use fountain pens. He told me to ring him if things didn't improve when I was finally discharged.

I slipped the piece of paper into my dressing-gown pocket and the nurse wheeled me out into the bright waiting-area.

Tracey wheeled me to the lift. I walked the last bit. We didn't say much. There wasn't much to say.

Two teenage student nurses are seated at the big table in the middle of the ward filling in their patient-progress forms. I have seen the kind of things they write about me –

'Ben is a well-kempt gentleman and his pain management has gone smoothly this morning.' 'Ben sat up and ate a piece of toast this afternoon.' 'Ben produced two stools of loose consistency, vomited and partook of light conversation.'

They look like they could be revising for their GCSEs. It is after lights-out. They are talking in hushed voices.

'Gary gave me a tape after the party. Loadsa music on it. Really good.'

'Oh, tell me. Like what?'

'Well, mainly The Waterboys.'

'Who?'

'The Waterboys. You know that Mike Scott bloke. The hat. "Whole of the Moon".'

'Oh, yeah, yeah . . . 'course.'

'And then there was this stuff by this other bloke on the other side. Really good. I mean really, really good. Sort of doomy but amazing words.'

'Who's that then?'

'Never heard of him before. Leonard Cohen.'

'Leonard Cohen. Oh he's really old. From the sixties.'

'Never is!'

'I'm telling you, he is.'

'How old.'

'Oh, ancient. In his forties. Must be.'

★

Occasional parties would be thrown over in the Queen Mary's nurses home on Saturday nights, largely attended by freshers or end-of-year leavers. Doctors and consultants would get ribbed in the days running up: 'Gonna strut your stuff, sir?' 'Get on down, Dr Brown!' And from nine until midnight the dull thud of kick-drum and sub-bass would pound quietly across the gardens. The nights would begin with reasonably up-to-the-minute club music but spiral downwards from then on through Abba and The Police until the last half-hour turned into a shapeless free-for-all when strains of oldies would float through the open window behind my bed – 'Dreadlock Holiday', 'Hit Me with Your Rhythm Stick', 'Layla', 'Y.M.C.A.'

I watched the younger nurses on St Mark's come in for the day shift after the weekends. They'd always get in just in time, like at school, scuffling and skidding into the ward for the morning update, leaving their identities at the door – rave DJ, crusty, swot, homebody. Accessories denoted allegiances. Dub-plate and twelve-inch shoulder-bag, nose stud, nurses handbook, bicycle clips. Some took to the job like ducks to water, able to submerge their egos beneath their work, or – better – merge them seamlessly into their patient-relationships. For these nurses, nothing ever seemed too much trouble. Kindness and patience seemed to flow naturally. Everyone liked these nurses.

Others struggled with themselves and seemed to find it hard to give. Their personalities would chafe against the day-to-day mundanity of many jobs – especially the relays back and forth to the sluice with bottles of piss. The irrational behaviour and sometimes wild knee-jerk accusations of neglect from the patients rubbed up badly against their own adolescent intolerance.

They had a need to assert themselves. It would manifest itself in little huffs as they turned away from the bed, deliberately clipped and swallowed speech, apathy or bullishness, subtle levels of inappropriate response. I really hated one or two of them some days, and I know they really hated me back some days too.

The next morning I wanted to walk somewhere. I was becoming more and more mobile as the days went by. I offered to fetch a paper for anyone who wanted one from the shop in reception. Lots of winking and the handing over of small change preceded my departure and, stooped over, I pottered off with my drip-stand and a pocketful of coins. I took my time. It was a trip out after all. I smiled at people in the corridors, kept the lift door open for doctors and patients in wheelchairs, and generally was as charming as I could be in my role as a rather emaciated, bearded Quasimodo.

Reception was buzzing. I queued behind nurses buying lunch – cheese roll, crisps, Lilt, Snickers – and paused by the huge granary baps stuffed with ham and salad, poppy-seeded subs crammed with egg mayonnaise, crusty baguettes of sliced turkey. Strangely, I didn't really crave them, in spite of not having eaten properly for weeks, but viewed them with the interest I'd give to arresting museum exhibits.

I asked for seven newspapers and bottle of Volvic. I got a carrier bag and hung it on my drip-stand and shuffled off. The place was vibrant. I loitered for a couple of minutes just watching. A pregnant woman was crying, her hand held by a little boy in full Batman outfit. He had on the cape, and the black mask with the hood and with the little pointy ears. An old man sat on his own with a walking-frame and a white plastic bag printed with the words 'I Ran The World'. A girl spilled a tube of Smarties all over the floor and they scattered like ball-bearings. People waited on a line of chairs for prescriptions, and nurses hurtled past as lift doors started to close.

I took the lift all the way to the seventh floor and got out into the empty corridor and pushed open the doors to the chapel. Tracey told me she had been up there when I was unconscious. She didn't really know why. Some restlessness. It was lonely and dry and lifeless. Heavy oak panelling lined the room. A huge oil-painting hung above the altar. There was no natural light. The carpet muted my footsteps. I felt my presence wasn't registered. I stood for a moment, but no thoughts came. I don't know what I was expecting, but the austerity was suffocating. I took the papers back down to the ward.

When I got back, a man was cleaning under my bed. The cleaners made the tea and washed the floors. Almost all the women on the staff were black. They wore bright yellow nylon dresses and would clack around in hard wooden sandals, languorous, taking their time. In the mornings one of them would bring fresh jugs of iced water and clean plastic beakers. Hot, weak tea came round with Marie biscuits at around eleven, and again at four. In between, the women mopped floors and changed the waste-paper bags by our beds. They chatted to each other in thick, accented language. The men who swept the floors and damp-wiped the surfaces seemed to be mainly from the eastern Mediterranean – Italian, Cypriot, Turkish, maybe. They wore blue nylon trousers with yellow Marigold washing-up gloves. The man cleaning under my bed had a feather duster.

'Hello,' I said.

'Hallo.' He looked surprised.

'How are you?'

'OK.'

'Where do you come from?'

He paused. 'Tunisia.' He stopped dusting for a moment. 'Harlesden now.'

'Really? How long have you been here?'

'One years.' He started running his duster over the wall.

'What do you think?'

'OK. Bad food.'

'Oh? What do you eat?'

'Lemons. Lemons and bread.'

'That sounds healthy. I eat this.' I pointed to my food drip.

He smiled. 'I think I like lemons in Tunisia better.'

'Me too.'

SIX

Two p.m. I am slumped on my bed. I have no strength. I see the same image of the bucket coming up dry again that I saw down in the garden on my first weekend on the Coronary Care Unit. Metal. I feel I have got something metallic in my mouth. Like I have just licked a coin. I started on a new course of oral steroids this morning, and it is a day after the cyclophosphamide. Has something gone wrong? Have the drugs done something bad? I was doing so well. I keep scraping my tongue back and forth under my front teeth to remove an imaginary film. My eyes feel dry and crispy. Dry autumn leaves. I screw them up, trying to get them to moisten. Dry crunched-up leaves. Broken veins and capillaries. Leaf veins. Like the back of a hand with a torch shone through it. I don't want water. I don't want to move. If I just lie here my mind will eventually wander and, before I know it, fifteen minutes will have passed and I might feel OK. My gut feels rotten. Trapped pockets of air and gas. A dachshund made by a balloon-twister. My head is an empty box. My thoughts rattle around, dry crumbs in a kitchen drawer.

Six p.m. I am on a lightly rolling ship. I can't talk. My stomach slops with bilge-water. My nose is full of nausea. Fumes on a car-deck. Oil. Burnt petrol. My ears hum with the drone of low engines. My eyes are opaque plastic windows, salt-blasted, unclear. Don't touch me. Deep breath.

Nine p.m. I am lying on my side. A waste-pipe running into the

sea. Effluence. Warm effluence. Backing up. I am concrete. I am
corrugated. The daylight has gone. The sea is black. I am spilling. I
am trailing along the seabed. I sit up. My stomach lurches and flails
like a dropped hosepipe coursing with water. I grope for the grey
cardboard bowl under the bed and I throw up. Green bile.

That night a nurse rolled me over and gave me a Paracetamol
suppository to bring my temperature down. I was feeling bad
and strange. I asked for extra blankets. I had taken to sleeping
on top of my bed, to keep as many layers between me and the
plastic undersheet as possible. I pulled a couple of white cotton
blankets over me. It was snug. I laid the pillow-rest flat and
managed to lie half on my side with my knees up. Sleep came
deeply and fitfully.

I dreamed of weevils and termites, burrowing into trunks
of wood, leaving them hollowed and pitted like cork. I was
stumbling, kicking over little hillocks and mounds of earth.
Hundreds of weevils were running over my slippers. My tubes
and lines were trailing through the earth. I tried to hitch them
up, but I could see insects already in the necks of the tubes,
like wasps climbing into bottles. I tried to shake them out, but
they were inside, running up the inside.

At 6.30 a.m. a nurse took my temperature. It had climbed
to 39.1. I rolled back into my pillows and watched breakfast
come round. Dry white sliced bread was on the trolley,
which meant the toaster was broken again. Cornflakes. Tea.
Powdered coffee. At least the milk jug was cold. I missed
breakfast a lot. My head felt like the rind of a fruit, juiceless
and extracted.

At eight the surgical team looked concerned. Everyone was aware of the dangers of the latest injection of cyclophosphamide. It had the potential to temporarily leave me with no defences. I was ripe for infection and my temperature was up. Maybe I'd picked something up already. They ordered a course of antibiotics, and a temperature reading every hour.

By nine it had hit 40. By ten it had climbed to 40.4 – about 105 degrees Fahrenheit. Nurses were gathering round my bed to watch the mercury rise. It was amazing in its frightfulness. I felt shrunken. I lay perfectly still. My head was a skull. My chin rested on my chest. Inside my head I felt the tissue was too small for the space it occupied. If I moved, it seemed to scrape against the surface. Abrasive. Stinging. Like grazing the fleshy part of the arm against a pebble-dashed wall. Twisting my head would bring out little electrical storms across my brow and down my nose and through my sinuses. Tiny lightning strikes. And I was a small creature who had made its home in this skull. Peeping out from the darkness. Tiny eyes like beads. Silent. Quietly scuffling in one of the sockets. I felt rotten in my guts. Nurses drifted in and out of my line of vision, often asking if I was OK. I didn't want to move my head, so I would just raise the corners of my mouth into a little smile.

At eleven I sat up and vomited again. As I sat up, my head came away from the pillow like Velcro. I was faint, light-headed. Two nurses were supporting me. They laid me down again. I closed my eyes. My stomach up to my mouth felt like a soft, hot pipe – pumping, fleshy, too big for my body. The sudden ascent of my temperature was leaving undisguised concern on the faces of the nurses. Two surgeons came back and ordered strong anti-nausea injections. They talked of another possible blockage in my guts from scar tissue or maybe another abscess. They arranged for an ultrasound scan for the following afternoon.

Paul, the houseman, appeared. More blood tests. Blood cultures were needed for signs of bugs and infection. Nobody really knew what they would find or what was really going on. I was deep into myself by now, insulating my responses, lagging myself against the unfolding crisis. My veins were sluggish and hard to find. Local anaesthetics were injected while Paul jabbed around in my arm. The tiny tube of the butterfly needle would spurt for a moment then stop as the vein failed to respond. He asked how I would feel about an attempt to draw blood from a big vein in my groin. I looked out of the window. I knew it was important. I didn't know what to say. I said OK. When he went in, it felt like a drawing-pin being forced into a stretched rubber band. The syringe filled instantly. I wanted to be sick.

I lay there in my dry skull for the rest of the day, dozing, not speaking. Tracey was there. I vomited again a couple more times in spite of the anti-sickness drug. Nurses would ask me if I was hot. I only felt dried out. Like something once damp, now shrivelled. A peach-stone. That night the electric storms started up in my face again. The worst since ITU. My temples buzzed with blood. I could feel my pulse beating all over my body.

By morning there had been little change. I don't remember the night passing coherently. Delirious dream landscapes. My temperature was still over 40. I felt crumbly, like parchment paper. Blood cultures had grown nothing. Without firm evidence of an infection, a blockage in the gut was talked about again.

At 2 p.m. Gert, the porter, collected me for Ultrasound. I was taken down in my bed, past the drawn faces of the X-ray out-patients in their gowns and towelling socks. The doctors tinkered around for twenty minutes, digging the scanner hard under my ribs. I fell asleep on the hard bed in front of them. They carried on scanning, running the scanner like a silent electric razor over and over my belly. The soft lighting. The grey quietness. The astronomy of ultrasound. I woke up. I wanted to stay and be swallowed up by something – another world of non-doing. Time-trapped. They found nothing, and a porter collected me.

Most of the rest of the afternoon I slept. The results of the ultrasound disappointed the surgeons. A yet undiscovered infection seemed likely again. It was decided my Hickman line should be removed that night, in case bugs were breeding in the warm milky food at the point where the line entered my chest, infecting my blood. A couple of hours later a young surgeon arrived to take the line out.

The curtains were drawn round. Hickman lines run deep into the chest. The longer they are in place, the harder it is to get them out. The skin tends to grow back around the entry site, binding the tube into the body. A heavy sedative was injected into my arm. My head lolled on the pillow. I went woozy. I thought I was about to be tattooed. A bluebird on my ribcage. And then I opened my eyes. Other patients were drinking hot drinks. *But hot drinks don't come round till late. My* chest was burning. I was alone. I looked at my watch. Two hours had passed. A nurse told me Tracey had stayed for a while but had had to go home. The Hickman line was gone and my chest was stitched with a strand of black thread. That night, if I moved, I felt like a hooked fish. The stitch seemed to snag. I had to sleep on my back, half sitting up again.

The next morning bled lifelessly out of the night before, grey, still, no patterns of sleep or waking. I was living on water only. I day-dreamed. Gentle hallucinations. Terracotta. I was made of terracotta. A clay oven, a brick, water and liquids evaporating off my surface, placed inside a wood fire. My temperature was still high. I lay still for hours. Every time I wanted to pee I had to call a nurse over. I wasn't allowed a normal urine bottle from the communal sluice. Each time the nurse had to crack open a sterilized plastic jug from a protective wrapper, wearing sterilized surgical gloves to minimize the risk of further infection. Everything I was emitting was being measured, recorded, analysed, tested. Amount, colour, consistency, viscosity, smell.

Mid-morning brought firm news at last. Something had been grown from my blood cultures. It seemed like I had some kind of blood poisoning – fungal septicaemia.

Everyone was relieved that there was at least a reason for all this suffering. My weight was plummeting. I'd lost ten pounds in three days. I was down to nine and a half stone. There had been talk a few days ago that I was almost ready to go home, but this latest set-back had distressed everyone. Pharmacy was alerted and a new drug was ordered. A fresh drip was rigged beside my bed in readiness. And when I looked up I thought I saw a sail on a mast and called a nurse over to tell her.

The new drug, an antifungal bombshell called Fluconazole, was dropped at midday. My body retreated further into itself, pulling back into trenches deep and familiar, leaving me half soundproofed from the hospital boom. I fell into a deep sleep. I dreamt I was draining away, water from an outdoor pool, leaves caught in the net above. And, as the water drained, the pool tiles were more chipped and scarred than anyone had ever imagined, so refracted and softened had they been by the soft lapping of life. I opened my eyes. I saw Tracey. The bedside table. Ribena. A beaker. I closed them again. I was dripping wet, my fever half sweated out, and I felt as though silt and stagnant droplets were on my mattress. A puddle. Midges hovering in a sweat haze over the filmy water. I thought I was by a roadside, beaten up, pushed out of a moving car at speed, face down in the verge of tall, dry grass and then rolling down the bank into the gully until I was face up in the filmy water.

I opened my eyes some time later. Like a dried dishcloth pressed into the shape of a clenched fist, I lay awake. It was late afternoon. My temperature was down. I felt at sea. On land, but at sea – the way the body can still sense the rocking of the boat for an hour after reaching the shore. I sat up for the first time that day and vomited. Pale-green liquid filled the bowl. Like lime cordial. It was good. As though my body was taking action. I felt I'd come back from somewhere. The worst was over. Tracey was still there. Had she ever been away? She pressed her hand against my forehead. Human contact. I felt the curve of her ring.

★

We spent our first night away together in Scarborough. We used to catch the train up to Bridlington or Scarborough and spend the days roaming the beaches and the back streets, eating chips and sitting in cafés on the front with pint mugs of tea, watching the hard winds whip in off the North Sea. We stayed at Mrs Thorpe's guest-house. It was May 1982. Both nineteen. Two Adults Bed and Breakfast £6 per day. Total £12. Paid With Thanks. Rough wool carpet and red linoleum in the room. A plate of Rich Tea and a kettle on the sideboard in the hall when you came in after 9.30. Tinned tomatoes, circular fried eggs and boiled button mushrooms in brine for breakfast.

We walked round the landscaped lake at Peasholm Park and along Marine Drive and down on to the beach as far as Scalby Mills and rode the out-of-season Astra Glide in overcoats, and then climbed up to the deserted castle and across the freezing headland to the Roman signal station and the ruined chapel by the cliff edge, the keep and bailey behind us. I can't remember anything we said, only the sea and the grey clouds and the racing winds. I can still see the outline of the priest's house alongside the chapel, the threshold and step to the door-opening at the west end opening into nothing but sky.

In 1969 one of my dad's last major jobs before he thought about packing it all in was a summer season at Scarborough. His love was big bands – big, bluesy, Basie-style – and nobody wanted them any more, except for tea dances. Any TV or radio work was always a compromise. He did thirteen weeks as MD of the pit band for Tommy Cooper at the Floral Hall. He says it was the funniest three months of his life. It was a punishing routine – six nights a week, plus an additional Sunday concert while Cooper, who would hire a private jet to fly south for twenty-four hours, was at home with his feet up.

He remembers watching the first Apollo moon landing in Tommy Cooper's hotel room. He was sitting on the edge of the bed with Cooper's wife while Cooper himself was stretched out in the next room on a special oversized bed like a catafalque calling out for action updates –

'What's happening in there?'

'Not a lot.'

Two minutes later.

'What's happening now?'

My dad stayed up all that time in a small room at the Station Hotel – a pub really. It was a real turf pub. York races. He picked a lucky Piggott yankee one afternoon, and from then on became known as someone worth touching on. Mum would visit. I went up once with her. We stayed out at a country hotel in the Forge valley called the Hackness Grange. I thought it was fantastic. Cooked breakfast and a pool.

In the evening I was allowed in the orchestra pit during the show. My dad was involved in a couple of routines, one involving catching a plastic replica bowling-ball as it bounced off Cooper's foot from the stage, which made me laugh. I clacked round the backstage corridors in a pair of Will Gaines's tap shoes, knocking on doors and watching The Square Pegs from the wings, wondering what a barber-shop quartet was.

Two years later we went down to the Bournemouth Winter Gardens, where my dad did one more season. He was just playing piano this time. There was a mixture of comics filling the weeks until the Bruce Forsyth season started. Freddie Starr.

Ted Rogers. Top of the bill when I was there were Hope and Keen. I played crazy golf in the afternoons and read the saucy postcards in the revolving stands outside the shops on the seafront, and then met my dad in the theatre canteen for beans on toast before the show and gazed at the chorus girls.

I went back to Scarborough with Tracey a couple of years after leaving Hull. It was 1986. We were on tour in the North and had a weekend off. It seemed romantic to go back. It was October and chilly, but beautifully bright and clear. The front was one long crescent of people catching one of the last sunny days of the year, pensioners mostly, in cardigans and sun-glasses with ice-lollies and binoculars. We had a bit of money by then, and booked in for a night at the St Nicholas Hotel on St Nicholas cliffs. Three-star, with a grotto leisure club. We felt quite up-market, although the hotel staff rather looked down on us. I had, it must be said, dyed my hair peroxide blond at the time. All the same, I played snooker in the lounge to show off and then paid in cash.

Arnold has gone from the bed opposite. His children took him home. Leslie has arrived. He seems to know all the nurses. He is very pale, but chirpy. He is wearing a light-blue anorak and carrying a little vinyl holdall. He pulls the curtains round his bed himself, changes, and has pulled them back again and is lying on his bed in his crisply ironed light-blue polyester-mix pyjamas before the nurses have even got back. He pulls a book from his bag. It is a Western. He smooths his fine and immaculately combed white hair down over his head as he reads. He spends a long time on every page, sometimes even turning back a page to reread something.

A houseman arrives. 'Come for your top up, Leslie?'

'Yes. Four pints of gold top, please!'

Leslie, it turns out, is anaemic. He is very patient. He is very pale now I look at him closely — almost see-through, like a phantom. The veins on his skin are like little rivers frozen over.

His blood-bag doesn't come up from the laboratory fridge for five hours. He stops the houseman as he passes through. 'I don't want to be a nuisance, but I'm hoping to be in Devon on Monday. On my holidays. Any chance . . . '

'I don't see why not. What's the problem?'

'Well, each bag takes eight hours and we haven't even commenced yet.'

'Right. We'd better get cracking then.' The houseman turns quickly.

Leslie stops him unexpectedly. 'I didn't want to disturb you from your engagements.'

'Sorry?'

'Your schedule. I don't want you to feel I am disrupting your busy schedule and the day-to-day necessities.'

'The what? Oh, don't be silly, Leslie.'

'I know how hospital affairs can impinge, and being only a non-crisis day admission . . . '

'Yes. Look, I'd better check on this blood.' He gets away this time. Leslie sits back on his bed with his Western.

A nurse arrives with a dinner menu. 'Will you be eating on top of your transfusion?'

Dr Mackworth-Young, my rheumatologist, arrived in the early evening with news that my eosinophils were responding well to the cyclophosphamide, indicating my immune system was generally dampened down. He was sorry about the septicaemia. He had a gentle bedside manner and blond hair that sometimes looked slept-on from the back. He wore old-fashioned clothes, but of immense quality. Derby boots. Leather Oxfords – Church's, probably. Pinstripe wool suits. Waistcoats. Collarless white shirts with separate collars and brass studs. His senior registrar, Rod, who often came too, was younger and handsome, with the bearing of a triathlete. I expected to find out he did extreme skiing or rock-climbing on his days off. He wore a diver's watch. Like his consultant, he had winning blue eyes, but not soft and pale and nursery-book, more vivid and holiday-brochure Aegean. He wore modern striped blue shirts to match. They made a good team. How much is reassurance part of recovery?

They had brought me a name for my illness too, having finally settled on a full diagnosis. Tissue-analysis tests had confirmed it as an autoimmune disease called Churg–Strauss Syndrome, an extremely rare disorder seen in individuals with a background of asthma and hay fever whose immune systems unpredictably and violently respond after further, but not necessarily related, antigenic stimulation. The result, as the immune system's antibodies battle overactively with the irritant in the body's connective tissue (in my case, most likely an allergen connected with my asthma), is wrecked blood vessels and interrupted blood supply (vasculitis), causing potentially fatal organ death. The immune system then roller-coasts out of control and begins no longer to recognize the body's own tissue, producing antibodies that start to devastate that too – hence the term 'autoimmune': literally, 'antagonistic towards oneself'.

The critical moment is characterized by the appearance of massive numbers of the immune system's marshalling forces (hypereosinophilia). Not only is the disease itself rare but the fact that it had chosen to settle in the tissue around my small intestine is rarer still. Most of the few known cases have been seen in the lungs.

It turns out that a history of asthma going back as far as childhood is uncommon. While it is one of the initial stages in the syndrome, asthma usually develops after the age of twenty, largely in young men. The gap between asthma and onset of the life-threatening vasculitic stage averages out at about three to five years, all of which fitted my pattern. So many of the debilitating symptoms I suffered in the first six months of 1992 are typical of the disease too – fatigue, muscle pain, arthritic pain, fever, hypertension, hoax heart scares, and a sudden improvement in the asthma in the run-up to the life-threatening phase after a noticeable bad downward trend. To paraphrase Joseph Heller, 'You know it's something serious when they name it after two guys.'

The next two days passed in a seamless stretch of time. I floated on the surface of the day-to-day activities of the ward, lying down to sleep and rest, sitting up to vomit. The early blood cultures were matching the later ones, and fungal candida had been found on the tip of the Hickman line that had been removed from my chest. It had, as suspected, got into my bloodstream via my liquid food. With enough evidence to discount an alternative source of infection, my antibiotics were finally stopped, and for good measure the antifungal drug was doubled. I was encouraged to eat and drink a little again. The doctors were concerned about my weight.

Nurses would come round in the afternoons, sit me up on the edge of the bed, wait for me to vomit, and then help me on to the weighing-chair. Stripped down to my pants, I looked like an enfeebled bantamweight boxer at a bottom-of-the-bill weigh-in. That evening I fiddled with a cheese sandwich and dribbled tomato soup off the spoon and back into the bowl until it was cold.

My body started calling for sugar. I got a craving for lemonade, and one of the housemen told me old-fashioned lemonade used to have traces of quinine in it, which was supposed to aid digestion. I sent Tracey out on a search for original R. White's Lemonade. She scoured the local shops but could only find modern brands. I took a bottle anyway, and guzzled two whole glasses chilled with ice the following afternoon before bringing it all back up in one long, hilarious, foaming, bubbling white chunder an hour later. The next day I tried another glass of lemonade at 6.30 a.m., after the early-morning drug round. It came straight back up. I tried a bowl of cornflakes at eight, and that too returned immediately. Suddenly things seemed more serious. The Prof began talking of a blockage again on top of the septicaemia. He ordered another barium meal.

Little in the ward distracted me during those days. It was the illest I'd been since ITU. It wasn't until a man arrived in the bed opposite to have his pile removed that I really took much notice. He was due up in theatre that morning, but there had

141

been a delay and he had already had his pre-med. It was one o'clock, and he was so stoned he couldn't stop laughing. The man in the bed next to him was talking to him.

'Are you all right, mate?'

Giggling.

'Mate, are you all right?'

Tittering.

'Shall I call a nurse?'

More giggling. He was lying on his side like a little boy in bed on the morning of his birthday, likeable, charming, face pushed up into the pillow.

'You won't be laughing later, after they've tied a knot round it and it's dropped off.'

Open laughter. The whole ward was laughing. One of the nurses was stifling a smirk and trying to tell him theatre was sorry for the delay. 'The porter will be down in ten minutes.'

'Arseholes he will.'

It was pointless. A wave of good humour was rippling round the room. It made me think of Sid James and Bernie Bresslaw and Hattie Jacques and striped flannelette pyjamas. We were all laughing and smiling while trying not to laugh, grimacing with the pain of bruising and stitching. It was the best feeling in the ward for weeks.

The porter arrived with a trolley. 'All set, then?'

We all collapsed. The man was helped on to the trolley. He was still sniggering to himself. As the porter and the nurse tried to lay him down he kept sitting up, pursing his lips and blowing air out in a weak raspberry. The porter cottoned on, and the whole party – the porter, the patient and two nurses – passed out of the ward on their way up to the operating theatre in a mini-pageant of tittering and clanging oxygen tanks.

The next day he was back on the ward. He was up and walking around. Still smiling, he looked as though he had got an egg clasped between his buttocks. Earlier on he'd been for his first crap since the operation. He'd come back looking startled. Expecting to see the residue of his last meal floating below him, he had looked down and saw, as I heard him describe to the man in the next bed, 'a bloody great big piece of bandage in the pan'. They then spent the next half-hour talking about it.

'What I want to know is, How did they get it up there?'

'Search me.'

'I couldn't believe it. I thought I'd eaten the wrapper off something.'

'I bet you feel better for it, though.'

'Not half.'

'Was it a big 'un? Did the doctor say anything about it?'

'Like a conker, mate.'

The day I felt stronger again, Tracey suggested a walk across to the TV room. It was only fifty-two paces away. It took a while, but we got there and I tried watching a nature programme. I was slumped into one of the TV room's toffee-brown leatherette sofas with so little support in it that I was folded up like a half-open jack-knife, so low down my knees obscured my view of the TV screen, like in a dragster or a hot rod. The drip-line in my arm was pulled a little too tight. The stand was too far away and I couldn't reach it to move it. I couldn't be bothered to move again.

There was a commotion outside the door and a family came in – mum, dad, daughter, son and grandad. They sloped in and all tetchily fell into the other leatherette sofa. Grandad sat near me on a chair, in slippers that looked like they had been made from bus-seat upholstery. Mum was wearing a pink sweatshirt with a sequinned pink panther on the front and a towelling shell-suit. Her face was tired and drawn. No make-up. The colour of porridge. She spoke in a kind of hissing shout.

'Stop that!'

'What?' whined the little boy. He was stabbing his sister with the ring-pull off a can of 7-Up.

'You know very well what.'

'What?' he whined again.

'Tell him to stop, Mum.' The little girl, older than the boy, was not really being hurt but saw an opportunity to get him into more trouble.

'Once more and I'm telling your dad!' hissed Mum.

It was not as though Dad was unaware of the situation. He was, after all, sitting right next to them all, but he was currently mute and staring vacantly at the TV, absent-mindedly tapping himself on the head with a rolled-up copy of the *Mirror*.

The little boy stopped and, with his ring-pull, started trying to slice strips into the arm of the leatherette sofa instead.

'Can I get a Pepsi?' the girl asked, without taking her eyes off the TV.

'No, you can't,' said Mum.

'Plea . . . se'

'No. You've got a drink.'

'Plea . . . se. It's only downstairs.'

'I said no.'

The little boy joined in. 'I want a Pepsi too.'

Suddenly Dad snarled. He made me jump. 'Shut it. All of you. Can't you see there is a man here who wants a bit of peace and quiet.'

Christ, he means me! I kept my eyes on the TV. Tracey was looking straight ahead too. Everyone went quiet. I felt very English and just ignored the comment. My arm was tugged. I thought it was going to be Tracey telling me it was time we went, but it wasn't Tracey and the sticky tape across my wrist holding the cannula in place started to stretch and pull.

'Dad!' Mum shouted.

Grandad had got up and was walking across the room. He was walking straight through my drip-line. He hadn't noticed. He kept going. I kept thinking he must stop, but he was like an athlete breasting a sagging tape. The drip-stand was starting to roll towards me, and I was being pulled out of the sofa.

'Dad!'

Tracey started to get to her feet.

'Look out!'

Grandad looked up and stopped in his tracks. He looked down. Without a word, he sighed, grunted, stepped back, and decided to sit down again. I eased back into my seat.

'Prat!' said Dad under his breath.

No one said sorry. Tracey sat back. I stared at the TV. She stared at the TV. We should have left right then but it would have seemed pointed, and anyway if we were going to leave our moment had been five minutes before, just after they'd arrived. It could have seemed like we were just going anyway.

We'd blown it. I caught Tracey's eye in my peripheral vision. Neither of us stirred. We were pinned in our seats by the Englishness of the moment, and plumped for trying to seem undisturbed and natural. I tried to feel the cannula in my arm without drawing attention to it.

'Can we turn over?' The little girl was getting restless.

'No we can't.' Mum again.

'Please.'

'No.'

'This is boring.'

'The man wants to watch it. He was here first.'

Me again. Please don't drag me into this.

'It's boring. I want a Pepsi. Can I get a Pepsi now? I'll use my own money.'

Dad exploded. 'Right that's it. All of you. Out. Come on – out.' He rapped his son on the head with his newspaper. The boy started to cry loudly. Really loudly.

I knew it. I knew it. We should have quit while we were ahead.

'Arrrghh! Mum! Mum! He hit me. He hit me.'

Mum was bristling now. She turned on her husband. 'You brute. What would Nan say if she could hear us all squabbling in the hospital where she's at death's door?'

'She probably could hear you with all the noise you're making. Come on. We're going.' He levered himself out of the sofa.

'I'm not going with you in a mood.' She folded her arms and sat back. Both kids were crying now.

'Look,' said Dad. 'There's a bloke here trying to watch . . .' He gave up. 'Just come on. Up. Out. All of you.' He gestured to them all.

They all got up. He ushered them towards the door like a farmer shooing sulky geese, while we stared at the TV like nothing was happening.

My fever responded well to the antifungal therapy. The barium from the second meal started to come through. The commode was full of it. It looked like Key Lime Pie. Within another forty-eight hours my temperature had stabilized one degree above normal. I was fed vitamin syrup, which made me puke, and iron tablets, which didn't. I was anaemic and under-nourished, but the Prof was worried I had spent too long in the hospital and seemed in danger of becoming soft-boiled, hospital-ridden, dependent. I know he had been hoping to discharge me a lot earlier had things not turned out so unluckily. He thought I should try some time at home, and so on the Friday of the August bank holiday, with my weight at only nine stone four and barely on my feet four days after a massive blood infection, he said causally that if there was no deterioration in my condition by the following morning and my temperature stayed down I could go home for the weekend. He left. I just stared at the ceiling.

That night new pains began in my chest and lower back. I couldn't twist or sit up. Paul, the houseman, was on duty. He was on a ludicrous shift, expected to be on call in any emergency for a mind-numbing forty-eight hours. He had just gone to snatch an hour's sleep. I didn't really want to disturb him. He worked hard. I liked him. The pains got worse across the base of my back and over the front of my ribcage. I lay still for another hour, until I couldn't breathe without discomfort, and then said I ought to see someone. Paul arrived ten minutes later. He said it could well be muscle strain from my trial walk on the stairs earlier in the day, but he wanted me to go down to X-ray straightaway to check for shadows. It was 2 a.m. on the eve of my possible discharge. I didn't want to think about home any more. I was collected by a porter.

The corridors were quiet and the lift was cold. I was taken to X-ray down in Accident & Emergency. The Page Street department was closed for the night. Down in the dim back corridors on the ground floor the last thirty years seemed to have passed unnoticed. No major redecoration could have taken place for years. The fittings were utilitarian and coldly functional. Bare bulbs in steel-grey pendant tin-hat shades hung from high, shadowy ceilings. Colours were muted and dull. Signs were illuminated by low-wattage lights. Pale milky-white letters. Black pipes. It made me think of wartime, pallid skin and death. We passed a couple of the night admissions. Blood-sprayed Air Jordans showed from under the curtain of a silent cubicle. An Italian was trying to get into the service lift. He was lost, looking for his daughter. The porter had to stop him and point in the other direction.

In the X-ray room I could barely move. I stood up from the wheelchair and gripped on to the chest X-ray periscope, a sickly koala on a tree, and then I was eased down on the hard trolley for abdominal films.

'Breathe in and hold it there.'

I took a shallow breath. The machine clicked hard and buzzed.

'And breathe normally.'

The X-rays showed up nothing. Back upstairs I slept a little after a shot of Voltarol.

In the morning I felt in less pain. The Prof – amazingly – said I could still go home. I lay in the bed for a moment after he had gone, just looking round the ward, unsure of what to do next. My drips were gone. I could have called Tracey there and then, but I didn't. Instead I picked up my washbag and shuffled to the bathroom. I took a shallow bath and combed my hair. I spoke to myself out loud. I brushed my teeth. I dusted myself with talcum powder. I turned around. I was aware of every choice I made. Everything was self-conscious, super-real. All mobility seemed to come from a multiple-choice test going on in my head. Do I open the door? Do I stand here for another minute or two? Do I go home now? Is this how prisoners feel when they finally get to go home? I slid the door back and walked out to the phone to call Tracey.

'How soon can you come down?'

'Why? What's wrong?' She was immediately alarmed.

'Nothing's wrong. Can you come and get me? They say I can come home for the weekend.'

'What? Are you sure?' She thought I was woozy with drugs again.

'Yes. I saw the Prof. Honestly. How long can you be?'

'I don't know. An hour. Look, are you sure? I'm only just up. I'm just having some toast.'

'Oh. OK. But come soon. See you soon.'

'OK. Bye. Are you sure?'

'Yes. Bye. Oh, can you bring me a belt for my trousers.'

And I put down the phone, the blue phone on wheels in the fourth-floor corridor, and looked down the corridor at the people in it, the strung-out teenager nurses, the languid service staff, the young, confident, overtired doctors and the creeping patients. I thought of moving and getting up, but instead I sat there for ten minutes just looking at the back of my hands.

I was worried about my main scar. It hadn't healed neatly. When the last set of staple clips had been removed a couple of days earlier it was clear that the two sides of my belly hadn't joined properly and a hole the size of a penny piece was opening under the strain. Seen from above, it looked like a Jammy Dodger. It was infected and had started to ooze a bit. One of the Prof's team had popped down to look at it and had pinched and poked it in a very casual manner. It was being dressed twice a day with salt-soaked non-stick seaweed dressing. I could never understand how it would join up again, but nurses told me that skin and flesh in the belly repair themselves differently from a cut finger, building up tissue and filling in the gap. I was worried about looking after it myself.

Tracey arrived. The clothes I had turned up in nine weeks earlier were brought up from the Patients' Property. Everything seemed huge. I felt like a tortoise in its shell – thin, wizened, reptilian, my neck thin, my head small. I felt as though I could start walking and be able to take half a step forward before my clothes even started to move. I thought of David Byrne in *Stop Making Sense*. I belted my trousers loosely at the waist, afraid of my gauze dressing and my funny belly.

Paul, the houseman, came up from pharmacy with a bag of

drugs to take home and told me to report back after the bank holiday. I felt like a soldier going home on compassionate leave. I said a few goodbyes, but I knew I would be back. Tracey took my elbow, and we just walked ever so slowly downstairs and out on to the street.

SEVEN

The house was a tall, dark box of bricks; no lights, no family at the door; a huge space in which, as I paused in the hall, I felt my thoughts go spinning and careering up the stairs one by one, ricocheting off the walls, pulling on the handrails, leaving fingerprints on the paintwork. The carpet smelt as I remembered. Underlay. Sea grass. It made me think of dust again. The kitchen ceiling was too high. The window out to the garden was smeary. Tracey had shuffled things into piles. Tidy but not tidy. So unlike me. There was washing-up for one by the sink, unwashed breakfast things for one on the table, a rented video ready to go back, take-away menus. It seemed a lonely place, a place kept on hold. Lifeless. In the emptiness we were arm in arm, Tracey's footsteps a patient copy of my Zimmer-frame moonwalk. I could hear her head fizzing like pylons, her thoughts like pinballs, crashing around under the glass.

We stood and just cried. Happy. Unhappy.

We went back to the hospital after the bank-holiday weekend. We got there at 7.30 a.m. to see the team on their morning ward round. I shuffled into the ward to get undressed and back into my bed ready for their arrival, only to see them all gathered round it. I was alarmed. What had they found? Were they waiting for me to tell me bad news? My palms tingled. And then I saw there was someone else in my bed and I wasn't on their minds at all, and I suddenly felt a painter being loosed and I was floating on my own, and the ward suddenly seemed big and not mine.

A nurse tapped me on the shoulder and we went over to the day-room. A little while later the team came over. I told them I was OK. I didn't know whether I wanted to stay or not. Home had been unrecognizable. Big, empty. I had crapped barium all though Saturday, slept on the little spare bed doped up with Voltarol and Ibuprofen on Sunday, and vomited back scrambled egg on Monday. My temperature had stayed down, though, and my white-blood-cell count was stable, so they said I could go home for good.

DISCHARGE LETTER

WESTMINSTER HOSPITAL
Horseferry Road, SW1P 2AP

Patient: Watt, Ben.
Date admitted: 27 June 92.
Date discharged: 1 September 92.
Diagnosis: Churg-Strauss Syndrome.
Operations/Treatment: 1 x diagnostic laparoscopy. 1 x diagnostic laparotomy. 4 x laparotomy and small-bowel resection.
Recommendations for Future Management: Small-bowel diet. Vitamin and iron supplement.
Domiciliary Services Requested: Nil.
Fitness for Work: I recommend that this patient remains off work for four weeks.

★

I ate wrong things for a while. Nobody knew what I was going to be able to eat, and the Dietetic Department was no real help. The single sheet of A4 from the dietitian was too depressing to look at and only told half the story: 'A low-residue diet avoiding foods rich in dietary fibre, the substance in plant foods which we cannot digest. Avoid all fruits. Avoid all vegetables, beans and nuts, wholemeal bread and high-fibre cereal.' It encouraged substitution with white rolls, cream crackers, corn-flakes, milk puddings and build-up drinks. Eat butter, eggs, large servings of meat, it said. Madeira cake, ice-cream, hot chocolate and evaporated milk. Nobody drew my attention to the fat content of these foods and the huge difficulty I would have in digesting fat, or to the fact that many vegetables and fruit are water-rich and therefore easy to digest. I ate far too much fat on my meat and too much dairy produce, often emptying my guts in one go, the shit sometimes rising above the water-line in the bowl like an atoll. Sometimes I would vomit back my last meal as it went down, and then smile at Tracey and say how much better I felt. It seemed natural. It was how I thought it was going to be for the rest of my life. I was just so grateful to be home. At one point I thought I was only going to be able to be at home for six days of every week, returning to hospital for a night of drips and drugs for the rest of my life.

I started on my long-term drug therapy aimed at controlling my immune system, involving slowly reduced amounts of steroids and immune-suppressants. My voice finally came back. I slept in the afternoons, shuffled round the house in big jumpers, let Tracey take my temperature every few hours, sat with hiccups for a while, spent long periods just sitting on the bog with my trousers down doing nothing. Thinking. Looking out into the garden. Comforted. Somewhere safe. My spine remained curved for a long time. Standing up straight seemed an unengineerable feat. My shoulders fell forwards. My arms seemed really long. My muscles and bowel and scar tissue ached and tore and stretched. I felt like an underweight fast bowler after the first practice of the season.

I dreamt of our house. Of the day we moved in. Almost a year to the day before I was admitted into hospital. And I dreamt vividly of the weeks that followed and all the building work. There had been dust in the air all the time. The banisters were permanently covered in a film of brick-dust and cement and plaster. I would wipe them down in the morning, and by the evening it would be back again. The carpets we had pulled up were matted with cat hair. Torn off corners of fibreglass cladding from the insulation panels lay on the floors in the basement like snagged sheep wool. The joiner said he wouldn't go in the same room without gloves and a mask. He said the particles of glass were so fine they got under the skin and into the lungs and never came out. I stood back and watched the sanding-machines throw up powder storms of shellac and wood shavings. At night I imagined the dust was in my ears, on my pillow, in the fridge. For three days we slept on a sofa-bed that had been stored in a removals firm's container on an industrial estate in the East Midlands. It smelled of damp and mustiness and wood smoke from the cottage where it had been before. One morning I tore out a fitted kitchen with my bare hands, ripping up cork tiles and sheets of hardboard, kicking out plasterboard panels that cracked in half leaving chalk lines of plaster on the walls and floors, and took off ceramic tiles with a chisel, chipping away until the stubborn ones crumbled or exploded in a puff of clay. When the fresh deep-pink plaster wouldn't dry out in the basement we used a dehumidifier to suck the moisture out of the walls. The rooms were airless and stuffy. I used to go and stand in them for a few minutes and scrape the fungus off the damp corners where the plaster met the brickwork. We wore dust-masks all day and opened windows, and I got out whenever I could. I kept an eye on my asthma, watching for any signs of deterioration, but it seemed unaffected, no different from usual. In the dream, though, I am blaming myself.

I told this dream to Dr Mackworth-Young. He said there was no reason to blame myself and it was too simplistic to try to retrospectively attribute my illness to one single moment. He said of course it was highly likely that the building work and renovations could temporarily aggravate an asthmatic, but there was no evidence to prove that they alone could precipitate life-threatening autoimmune disease. He said the world is full of hundreds of thousands of people who suffer from bad dust-related asthma who never ever develop anything else, and the fact that only a minuscule proportion of people does suggests that it is to do with something specific within those few individuals that, at a certain point in their lives, would respond adversely to *any* amount of antigenic stimulation. It is likely that I just have a predisposition for hypersensitivity in general, genetically configured or inherited. I could go and live on the top of a mountain, breathing in clean, fresh mountain air away from all pollen and dust, but I would quite possibly develop a new set of local allergies given time – all initially harmless but all in the end as potentially damaging when presented to my immune system at a given moment. Another doctor has recently pointed out I might as well blame myself for every time I have ever hoovered a floor or slept in an unfamiliar hotel bed. We come into contact with common allergens every day.

Looking back, I suppose I could point to similar moments that could have been a catalyst but weren't, suggesting that my final destructive response was indeed less to do with one big trigger and more a subtler combination of a genetic fault mixed with chance and bad timing. I have swept the soot out of industrial boilers as a holiday job, played long days of sport on freshly cut outfields right through my twenties, spent claustrophobic weekends in front of smoking wood fires, redecorated flats, lived and worked for two months in smog-filled Los Angeles, all with no immediate detectable adverse effect. So did any of these moments make any difference at all? It is like trying to answer whether the life experiences of a crazy person contribute to or cause their craziness or whether they were just crazy all along.

I still find I wonder about the last few tantalizing weeks before my hospital admission. The fatigue and fevers and palpitations suggested a body already in distress, but did those earlier winter weeks of increasingly strong antibiotics for unlikely chest infections weaken or disrupt my immune system at a critical moment? Did I in fact suffer one key viral infection, a common cold even, that tipped the balance? I think about the homeopath's tablets. If homeopathy works on the basis of administering a critical amount of that to which one is allergic to encourage the body to fight it on its own, did the tablets unwittingly light the touch-paper on an already volatile situation? I read an article recently about a woman who spiralled into fully blown autoimmune disease seemingly after ingesting Chinese herbs taken to combat her long-term worsening allergy. And what about my trip to Japan and its link with food poisoning? Ironically, some weeks after my hospital crisis was over, David Lindsay even revealed that, while most of the early parasite tests had come back negative, one had actually returned late and was inconclusively borderline-positive.

More broadly, heredity, environment and diet and their relationships to the aggravation of allergy are all areas of current popular fixation. I read and watch TV programmes about genetic markers, T-cell imbalance, plant spores, acid rain, car fumes, aerobics-induced lung sensitivity, household chemicals, English dust mites versus American dust mites, wool blankets, indoor pets, sealed living conditions, post-viral weakness, overdependence on antibiotics, mutant flu strains, dairy produce, additives, red meat – the list is endless, and in the end I can only conclude that some of us are gonna get hit and some of us aren't.

A bad day. I've been home a week. I can't sleep lying down because my back and belly hurt so much. I eat and then just fart all day, my guts heaving like sulphur pits and geysers where the crust of the earth is thin and hot, like some desolate Icelandic landscape. I eat and then vomit my food back undigested. I eat and then shit out the entire contents of my bowel, and watch them floating in the bowl like a sludge of ginger nuts or melted Caramac. I can't walk without cramps, or a permanent stiffness in my groin. My shoulders won't straighten. I walk to the shops with my hands instinctively hovering over my belly. I walk like prisoners walk whose ankles and wrists are chained to a central body belt, hunched forward, restricted. The small hole where my stitches haven't healed properly is oozing every day. I soak non-stick seaweed gauze dressing in warm salty water and fold it diamond-shaped with tweezers, and then leave it in the hole to help it heal, and watch daytime TV with the sound off. My hair is thin and lies flat, full of static. My scalp is dry. I use moisturizer on my head. My fingernails and toenails are too soft for scissors. I sit at the kitchen table and want to roar. I want to throw back my head and roar like a circus bear, but the tears won't flow properly. They seep out like water through rocks. My head is in my hands. Is this what grief is?

A good day. It is a wonderful Sunday morning. I stand crouched by the bedroom window. It is eight o'clock. My chin rests on my hands in full warm sunshine five storeys up with birds flying below me. I am thin. Still thin, even now, but today I don't care. I can get my hands round my thigh, thumb to thumb, little finger to little finger. I buy size small. I'm looking forward to the sales. It is always the small sizes that are left on the rail. Looking at Tracey, I know it's all different. Life stretches beyond me like a road to the sea. I don't want myself so much. I feel smaller. I keep my hair short. I leave things a little later than I used to, knowing that I might have a change of mind in ten minutes or so. I like my face very much. My eyes are very blue. I suit my clothes. I like my beard too. My hard, flat belly is unfamiliar. I *don't like to touch it. It is like a rocky desert – bumpy and dry. I proudly show off my scar to anyone who'll look, but on my own it frightens me. I hate TV. I can't watch it, except the sport. I think a lot. I follow planes across the sky in the morning. I watch the clouds blowing up behind the houses. I like sitting up in bed – sometimes in the late afternoon, letting the light go without turning the lamp on, or sometimes in the morning before Tracey is awake and the workmen have arrived at the building site, propped up in pillows and warm from a night's sleep. I feel alone but not lonely. And then I gently lie down again, have her roll away from me – 'Over, Rover' – slip down the bed a little way, and curl myself in behind her, knees up, a key in a lock.*

Four weeks after I was discharged I seized up at home. I was watching the Sunday match. I'd been feeling crampy since mid-morning. I thought it might have been hunger, so I had eaten some plain toast and a little lean bacon at noon. Sitting in the chair in front of the TV, I had felt my belly tightening. I got up and could barely walk. I slumped on the stairs. Tracey called a taxi. An ambulance would have only taken me to the Royal Free, and I had been told to get down to the Westminster in any eventuality. I felt faint, hot and cold. I wanted to clear my mouth of something. I was swallowing hard. It took me five minutes to get down one flight of stairs. I felt like I had done a hundred sit-ups for the first time in my life and woken up the morning after, stiffened, tied into a corset. The ride in the cab was cruel. Pot-holes and sleeping policemen shook me up. The journey seemed to be across one long cattle-grid. I was a goods train with no shock absorbers going over and over the same set of points. I crouched in the back, gripping myself still, eyes brimming with tears, staring at the backs of the fold-up seats in front, Tracey with her hand on my back, although I didn't want it there.

After three days of rest and fluids, on steroids and antibiotics in my old side-room on Marie Céleste, the pains had settled down. The cause was unknown. A passing infection maybe, or a blockage caused by healing scar tissue, or maybe a spasm caused by bad communications along the lengths of damaged nerve endings in the gut itself. The Prof wanted me to go to Charing Cross for a special test to check for hidden infection. I was to go up to the twelfth floor. The Department of Nuclear Medicine.

There was no ambulance to take me the next morning, so a local minicab was ordered. I sat in the back with Tracey, crawling through rush-hour traffic on the Cromwell Road, reading through the weeks of hospital notes I had built up. A floppy disc might have been easier to carry, but somehow the bulging folder I was taking with me seemed an appropriate expression of the sprawling size and seriousness of my illness. We pointed at the funny ink-pen sketches of my abdomen and the opinions marked by double question marks, filling the pages more like a suggestions book than a hospital file, and we laughed awkwardly at the early misdiagnoses, the endless opinions sought from department after department, the crossings out and the exclamation marks, and then we fell silent and sat staring at the cars.

Up on the twelfth floor, blood was extracted from my arm, the white cells separated, tagged with a radioactive marker, and then injected back into my arm to see where they would go.

If a hidden infection had been lurking in my belly, under a scanner the natural movements of the white cells towards the site of the infection could have been monitored on a screen – like the movements of migrating birds or whales. They sent me away for a few hours.

We sat in the open-plan coffee-shop on the first floor, drinking tea. Someone recognized us and came over to say hello and how she liked our albums. We didn't know her. I was grey, pale. What did she think of me? What must she have thought I was doing there?

A girl dressed in a theatre gown in a wheelchair next to me had no hair. It had all fallen out in clumps. Her skin was translucent like the moon, and yellowed like the pages of a book left on a shelf in the sun, but she seemed at ease and spirited. I felt momentarily close to her while all around me confused, internalized relatives ate sandwiches without a word.

The tests showed up nothing. Back at the hospital I sat fully clothed waiting for the Prof's evening ward round. I wanted to go home. I wanted him to think I was well enough. The pains had almost gone. He said OK – I think he thought it was pretty much all down to me now – and we slipped away into the night with no real answers. I was relieved and depressed.

A good night. The ball is floated in. Harford reaches for it. And . . . no, it's not going in. Wait . . . yes . . . it is bloody going in. Harford has gone and scored. The place erupts. We're at the back of the middle tier. Stamford Bridge is packed. The green, dewy, phosphorescent light from the floodlights picks the players out, dancing and embracing. The evening sky is indigo and mauve. I'm on my feet, screaming. I've only been out of hospital five weeks. Men are clasping each other in front of me. 'Mickeee Harrrford!' Tracey and Michelle are clapping wildly. I turn to my dad, on my left. He is still sitting down. And he is just looking up at me – looking up through his wire frames and smiling at me, with everything else going on around him.

After the game, we walked out of the ground through the thronging crowd and he held my hand like a child. He sixty-five, me twenty-nine. He is a small, gentle man. He seems smaller to me than when I was a teenager. Thoughtful, quieter, self-absorbed. He hasn't touched a drop since I came home. He wears little suede moccasin shoes. We pressed up towards the gate and I thought about the gulf between us in the hospital. The nights when I would say over and over to myself, 'Why have you withdrawn? Why have you retreated from all this? What world has taken you in, away from pain and facing me? Do I mean that much? Why won't you come? Why won't you stay? Weren't we once two oaks?'

Out in the Fulham Road we stood at the top of the stairs and said goodbye to Richard and Michelle and then there we were suddenly – me, him and Tracey, the three of us – with the people streaming past us and the city night surrounding us, and I felt momentarily in the lee of some great storm that we had all weathered, and how, for a moment during the weeks and weeks, we had lost sight of each other, but now we could see each other again.

A bad night. I find it hard to understand this bleak shaft that has been sunk into me. It is deep and dark. I extract nothing but self-pity and loneliness. The rock-face is hard. I sense the seam goes on and down for miles. I quarry my own thoughts. I come up in a cage with a pounding in my head, tired and small again. I despair. I am only young. I am not even halfway through my life. I can't eat what I want to eat. And if I eat too much of the little I am allowed I know the pains and blockages will start and an ambulance might have to come and take me back to the hospital. I wake in the mornings and instinctively push my fingers into my belly for the little signs that I have learnt to recognize. Sometimes Tracey catches me checking again during the day and I wish she hadn't seen me. I want us to remain special. Not careworn. In these post-illness days we have been given something that eats up too much time, feeding on our concerns, blind to our fatigue, like an unexpected baby with an infancy marred by illness and an uncertain future.

Sometimes I sit with her and describe my favourite meal with all its courses, and it is probably something I will never eat. We laughed a year ago and thought it wouldn't be long before I put on weight — friends always ask — but in fact I've lost more since I came home. And now I find I don't like photos of myself from two years ago or more. I don't like the fat young man I see — a fleshy boy, spoilt, clean-shaven — but nor do I like the pinched, hunched figure that stands before me in the mirror now. I know it is a man's body, but it is a man's body in distress. I don't really recognize him. For twenty-nine years I was overweight, and now I'm thin. I distrust my body so I live in my head, with the central heating on because I feel the cold so badly without an ounce of fat on me. And I hate it with the windows closed, because the air dries out and kitchen smells hang in the downstairs rooms.

I see our ever-so-slow shopping trips and mornings changing dressings, long silences and a strange new courtship where conversations drag over the same ground, trying to make sense of everything that has *happened, our words worn smooth by repetition and the cycle of recounted experience, and I don't know what to think any more.*

Four weeks after the first return to hospital I crashed again. My abdomen went into spasm. This time I tried to sleep it off, but the creeping paralysis woke me at 6 a.m. I was unable to swing my legs out of bed. I rolled out and huddled my crunched-up body into the bathroom and puked into the bowl. The trip in the taxi was bad again. I looked up and we were only on Haverstock Hill. The journey stretched ahead of me lamppost by lamppost.

I asked the driver to pull over on Whitehall. It was dim and grey, first city light, and I remembered winter mornings as a schoolboy on the edge of the common waiting on the corner by the Red Rover for the 72 or 33 with the South Circular thundering by. I stumbled from the cab and retched almost nothing into the gutter. I was by a bus-stop. A bus stopped. People watched me from the windows. A little boy rubbed away the mist to have a closer look. I was on a double yellow line. The taxi's hazards were strobing me like disco lights. The bus pulled away. Across the road was the Whitehall Theatre, where my godfather was an actor for years in the Whitehall farces. I leant on the taxi for a moment and felt as though my trousers could have been round my ankles and all of London was watching. And who was I to the two or three people who passed me by, and to the people on the bus? A sad drunk on his way home from all-night clubs and bars, inconsiderately throwing up at a public bus-stop like a dog? Someone not to be, anyway.

At the hospital Tracey found a wheelchair. I felt that if I didn't lie down I was going to pass out. I didn't care where I lay – the corridor, on the floor of the lift. We went straight up to the ward. They found me an unmade bed. The Prof came immediately. I wanted him to cut me open there and then. I was given pethidine again within half an hour, and soon I felt myself sliding away down a stainless-steel slide again into cotton-wool clouds until it was mid-afternoon, my knees pulled up, still in the T-shirt I arrived in.

The pattern was the same as before. Rest, fluids, drug-dulled sleep, antibiotics, steroids, no clear diagnosis, and then an improvement. I stayed in another couple of days. I'd already forgotten the feel of ward life, although the signs and little dramas all day long were familiar. I watched a girlfriend get up from the chair beside her partner's bed and, without really looking up from her magazine, flick and disperse the air bubbles that were stopping the liquid food in his supply line. She even knew how to reset the alarm that rang when it happened. Tracey used to do the same. A nurse didn't even bother to come over. I wondered if this was happening in all the wards. Like little car alarms all over the hospital.

An old man was out in his chair. He looked distraught and uncomfortable.

A young physio was talking to him. 'Come on, Mr Mildmay. This is the road to recovery. You have to try.'

He was upset. He must have been seventy-five, but his face was that of an eight-year-old. 'I can't. I can't move.'

'Come on, now. I'll help you up.' She took his elbow.

'I can't. I can't.'

There was something in the tone of his voice. Something pleading that drew everyone's attention and sided us with him against the nurse. How could she be so cruel? Couldn't she see the man was in pain and distressed?

She forced him onwards. 'Now then. Up we go.' She got him to his feet. He was whining quietly. 'Right. That's good,' she said. 'Now then, one foot forward, Mr Mildmay.'

Suddenly his face changed. He looked really anxious. His voice cut through the room. A voice of alarm. 'My leg. I can't move my leg. I can't feel my leg. It won't move. I can't move it. I can't walk.'

I wanted to look away. What had happened to this man? This was awful. Stop her someone.

'Mr Mildmay, the chair is caught on your pyjama trousers.'

'What?' He looked down.

She lifted the leg of the chair and freed him.

'Bugger me!' he said. And without another word he broke free of her grip and started pottering across the room.

For want of any clear evidence, healing scar tissue causing the uneven passage of food in the bowel became the favoured diagnosis for my latest, and also probably the previous, breakdown. Either that or gridlock from a gut temporarily stalled by bad nerve-ending communications or simply too much food to process. At least the problem seemed plainly mechanical, not disease-related, not the return of the danger-ous vasculitic stage of my illness; more a result of the funda-mental problem of living with such a short intestine. Within three days I was going home again.

★

My mum remained anxious for months. Every time I called I could hear her heart beating in her voice in her opening words, as though I was calling to say another ambulance was on its way for me. It stopped me from calling some days, even when I only had a good piece of news about nothing in particular. I couldn't bear to hear her anxiety. It was like listening to a creaking fault-line or earth tremors. I could hear her thoughts like tectonic plates shifting back and forth. The surgery and the damage to my gut were comprehensible to her, but the idea of self-mutilation from one's own immune system triggered by something as seemingly insignificant as an allergy was hard to fully understand. I'm sure now back at home she felt suddenly exiled and cut adrift. She fought to understand my new enforced diet, but I think she secretly hoped like everyone else around me that it was only going to be temporary and that soon I'd be eating like a horse and putting on weight. After all, everyone loses weight in hospital. She carries a sketch of my new resected gut in her handbag along with a picture of an unaffected gut and shows people when they ask about me.

I stayed over at their house on New Year's Eve. I sat at the top of the stairs in a vest and pants, waiting for my dad to finish in the bathroom, and she saw me and had to go outside, and I saw her crying on the towpath. She said she'd come on to the landing below and unexpectedly seen me like it was twenty years ago – I looked like her little boy again.

Some days I try to sit down and tell her everything, but I hear myself using a detailed scientific language that gets in the way, so other days I just put my arms around her without saying anything, as we stand in a doorway somewhere, and I tell myself, 'She was there. She saw it. Maybe that is enough.'

A week later my new car arrived. I saw it come down the street. A little red, gleaming Alfa Spyder. Two-seater. Right-hand drive. I had a stick to walk with. The young man from the dealer didn't look happy handing over the keys to someone looking so ill. He left casting a last look over his shoulder. The car seemed strange. An idea from another life. I had ordered it back in May, to be ready after our US tour, but within weeks I'd been admitted to hospital. Tracey had to pay the balance on it while I was sedated on ITU. There's faith for you. It looked like a toy out there among the Fords and the Volvos.

I stood looking at it out in the street from the kitchen window on and off for a little while, and then I said I wanted to drive it. Tracey said, 'You must be joking!' I said I only had to sit down behind the wheel. It wouldn't be too strenuous. Round the block or something.

Outside, the car was still ticking and clicking. I lowered myself in. It smelt leathery and plasticky. The suede inlay on the seats was buffed up to a buttery yellow, like clean chamois. There were still traces of clingfilm round the keyhole and on the levers of the quarter-lights. The carpets were unmarked, and droplets of water clung to the wing mirrors.

Fifteen minutes later we were at the foot of the M1 at Staples Corner, and without hesitating I pulled the car round past the Edgware Road turn-off, past the hitchhikers on the first corner of the hard shoulder, and, pressing my right foot richly into the floor, let the car accelerate up into the middle lane of the

motorway. Tracey was speechless. I eased the car over the first
incline and, as we levelled out, settled into a 65 m.p.h. slip-
stream behind a 5-series BMW, staying in fourth to hear the
high, tense growl in the engine. I thought of a cranked-up
Fender Vibrolux, 2×12, in brown Tolex with swell control,
its valves rich and warm.

'What are you doing!' Tracey was popping and spluttering
like a Roman candle.

'Just up to Scratchwood and back. Don't worry.' I could see
her holding on to her seat.

A few minutes later I slowed into the slip-road and took the
road round the outside of the service station, back over the
motorway, with views over the Hertfordshire fields, past two
police patrol cars and down the other side.

I felt low to the ground. The suspension was hard, the revs
high. The clutch was leapy under my foot. The gearstick
hummed in my hand. Wind whistled through the half-opened
vents and the cracks in the doors. I was exhilarated and I was
frightened too, but I didn't say it. And we were bubbles within
a bubble. In an egg. Eyes forward. Watching different versions
of the world fizzing by through a smeared windscreen. Speed.
Light. Sound. Memory. All the little things that keep us different and make us the same. And my hand was only six inches
from hers and I could have reached out and I know she would
have responded but I didn't, and I kept it loosely on the
gearstick and felt the tarmac hurtling away from under me.

EIGHT

Galway's damp, briny air is making Tracey's hair fall flat. We round a corner near the Spanish arch and a gust of squally air brushes my lips with salt. We pass along by the quay and upstairs into the quiet early evening of a restaurant, where we settle down to the last meal of our summer tour. Grilled sole, boiled potatoes, oysters and Guinness – low fat, low fibre.

It's July 1993, nine months since I left hospital, and in the past few weeks we have played seventeen concerts, touching all points of the local compass save the far south – Glasgow, Ipswich, Guildford, Galway.

My blood tests have been consistently good. I have reduced my drugs to less dependent levels, and the disease is currently showing no signs of returning. With it contained, in many ways I am left only with the shadow of the damage it caused, which is only what someone else might be enduring after major abdominal surgery following bowel cancer or a bad road accident or a shrapnel wound.

I marvel at the baroque descriptions in the final medical report of my hospital admission that I now carry with me – 'epigastric abdominal tenderness and mesenteric angina', 'multiple organ tissue eosinophilia', 'small-bowel ischaemia and infarction'. My gut locks up every few weeks, but I can deal with it now on my own without needing an emergency bed. The old hospital has closed. It has been merged into the new Chelsea and Westminster. It seems strange thinking of not going back there again if I ever need a bed. I think of the empty rooms quite a lot. Like a disused airfield.

So what do I eat with only 15 per cent of my small intestine left? Well I could begin with what I don't eat. No cheese, no butter, no oils, no eggs, no whole milk, no nuts, no pulses, no pasta, no chocolate, no cake, no crisps, no pastry, no biscuits, no brown bread, no greens, no lamb, no sausages.

So what does that leave? Well, lean grilled and roasted meats – chicken, venison, beef and turkey. Most grilled and poached fish except the oily ones like salmon, sardines and kippers. The insides of baked potatoes, or boiled spuds, white rice. Twenty-five per cent of my diet is made up from white breads. I eat vegetables with a high water content and low dark-green-leaf content – courgettes, depipped tomatoes, onions, lettuces, mushrooms. And low-pip mushy fruits – strawberries, grapes and peaches. Low-fat yoghurts and Frosties. Meringues are good. All the fat of an egg is in its yolk, none in the white. I drink skimmed milk, fruit juices and Coca-Cola. Sugar is my friend. I once spent £100 asking a top gastro-enterologist in Harley Street what improvements he could make to my diet, and all he could think of was boiled sweets.

I've learnt to use other rich flavours to make up for a Western diet's reliance on fat and oils – soy sauce, mustards, balsamic vinegar, honey, ginger and lemon juice, fresh herbs. Alcohol has become central. Other expert advice from a leading doctor recently was beer and brandy. High in sugar. High in calories. Alcohol is absorbed through the stomach, not the gut, and the rest is water. It's hard to beat a pint of Theakston's.

Of course the big drawback in all of this is quantity. Small portions. No snacks. Ironically, in some aspects it bears a resemblance to many common slimming diets, but it differs in its strict avoidance of fibre and exacts a high penalty for misjudgement of amounts. Spasms, colic, diarrhoea, enforced fasting. I keep a meticulous diet diary, balancing daily nutrients like an alchemist. My small intestine is now very abnormally shaped. I lost almost all my jejunum (the long middle part), the part that absorbs most of the goodness from food, but I have been left with the majority of my ileum (the lower part), which takes its time over any remaining food digestion and absorbs water and essential minerals in a slowing-down process. I suppose if I had to lose either I'm left with the better option. My colon, the large bowel, which tumble-dries the waste, is unaffected.

I hover around eight and a half to nine stone. Not a lot, I know, and proving to be almost impossible to improve upon without resorting to unacceptable measures like a naso-gastric drip feeding me liquid sugar or bucketfuls of high-calorie stir-ins — powdered glucose with supposedly no additional sweetness. I tried them and they just depressed me. My weight is stable at least. I wear twenty-eight-inch-waist trousers, having been a thirty-six and buy shirts in small not large any more. I once touched thirteen stone in 1989. I watch my friends ballooning into middle age.

I've started having nightmares. They are not frequent but always located in strange, unrealistic landscapes where I'm under pressure from childish monsters and outsized shapes and shadows. Often the narrative is similar — a situation where if people don't act on my behalf immediately I will be in serious danger, or worse: they cannot see the imminent danger I'm in, because it appears unthreatening to them. These dreams can cause me to shout out in my sleep, waking Tracey, or sometimes she will wake to hear me grizzling quietly and have to shake me gently awake. Are they spectres of all those unresolved days of non-diagnosis or the moments of anaesthetic and resection coming back to haunt me after all?

Occasionally I will sweat heavily in the night for no apparent reason. No rising temperature. No spike. No fever. Just some kind of a disturbance. I wake and think I have just had a bad dream, but cannot remember. Only the damp sheets point to one. Sometimes my temperature can drop instead, unexpectedly, and I can get the shakes and shivers and need extra blankets or a heating-pad to get me warm again. I will fall asleep under all the swaddling, only to wake roasting half an hour later. I prop myself up on pillows and lie awake, cooling down for forty-five minutes, listening to the pockets of air popping and puttering in my belly, the whining of the territorial tom-cats down in the neighbouring gardens through the open window, the clank of metal bins being filled behind the high-street restaurants after kicking-out time, or just the tick, hum, click of a house at night. But mostly my nights go by uneventfully, albeit in fits and starts – two hours here, three hours there. I sleep so lightly mostly, like I'm only just below the spun coating of waking and I could open my eyes and sit an exam at any moment. The drugs probably play a part in this, regulating and seeping and frothing through my body at night.

As for the cause of all this enforced change, I am told that with this illness I am at the forefront of medical knowledge in the fields of immunology and rheumatology. Until the late seventies and corticosteroid treatments most people with serious Churg–Strauss Syndrome died. Many of the defining features of the disease as outlined by Churg and Strauss in 1949 were discovered at autopsy stage. It is, needless to say, extremely rare. Thirty cases were reported in twenty-five years. Even in a major study at London's Hammersmith Hospital between 1976 and 1982 only sixteen contemporary cases were presented, to which a hundred or so other potentially but inconclusively related cases were added from medical literature. It should be said that these low figures are partly due to the narrow range of criteria needed to define the disease, and to the fact that most of the criteria appear in other related conditions, often deflecting a full diagnosis.

The future is largely unbroken ground, and no one can give me a truly confident prognosis. Blood tests will show the first indications of climbing eosinophils, pointing to unusually vigorous immune activity, so I go to the hospital every couple of months. I sit in the out-patients' clinic for my regular check-ups, with little old ladies in with their creaking knees, and read leaflets on the more common related conditions – lupus, rheumatoid arthritis – each of them centred like mine around a dangerous imbalance in the immune system.

My asthma has returned a little bit, but that is apparently common. With careful steroid and immune-suppressant treatment things look promising. Survival rate is up to 90 per cent now. There is even a chance of a full withdrawal from the drugs, but the disease would always be in the background and if it were to return its pattern might not even follow the same triggers. The same factors would have to be present – genetic quirk, a series of viral or allergic catalysts, blood abnormalities – but, like a mosaic, the same fragments could make a difference picture when placed side by side in a different order. All anyone will say is, 'With any luck . . .'

But I won't be held back. We played in London last week. Half the hospital came. Most of them hadn't seen me for almost a year. Dr Mackworth-Young was stunned. He could only ask Tracey how she remembered all the words. I find my voice has a new-found strength to it, a greater projection, more meaning. Does it resonate more in a hollower body? The sound is on a taut string, vibrating, humming like overhead electricity cables. It comes out of my mouth alive, and restless to communicate energy and understanding.

★

The room at the Ardilaun that night in Galway was packed. Chandeliers hung from the low ceiling. The festival atmosphere was strong and willing. We played our songs for an hour and a half. People clapped and drank. It was good.

A month after Galway – almost a year after I left hospital – we took a holiday. We flew to New York, took a train into Connecticut, and hired a car. The doctors said I might as well go for it, so I did. We drove to Cape Cod. It was early September. My skin tanned and stretched over my ribs like deck-chair canvas. My scars wouldn't change colour, not even the little ones on my wrists and chest. They stayed white, like marker flags on a playing-field. In the driving-mirror I noticed how I now have crow's feet in the corners of my eyes and the skin hangs looser on my cheeks even though the sun had tightened them and polished them up like a hazelnut. My eyes stood out from my face with the grey-blueness of sea views on clear November days on the Humberside coast. My face was like a new friend.

With Tracey beside me it was all too corny for words. On the American road. Babe in the front of a rented car. We couldn't stop smiling. Hospital taught me a new language with a different rhythm that goes on inside our heads all the time, a ceaseless stream and current of thoughts and words, babbling and pulling through all our waking hours. I learnt to listen to it, like listening to the sea from a bedroom window. At first you don't hear it, and then you realize that it is underpinning every sound, and it has its own rhythms and pulse. And it took me elsewhere, shell-less, into myself, where meaning came

176

from loneliness and calmness, acceptance, adaptability, gratitude and making peace with oneself.

But there in the car we were talking the old language again, and it was good. When Richard Ford said that love was transferable, I think he meant (with typical realist lyricism) from place to place and person to person, but it can also mean from time-of-life to time-of-life, deepened by change, in the same place with the same person. It is, I suppose, the shell on our shell-less back – a place to live in, to hide in, to carry with us, protection. Without it I feel we could all be nothing. Crushable.

'Enjoy yourself,' a doctor said to me before we left. 'You've not had the luck.'

It goes without saying that good and bad luck are only two sides of a flipped coin, but even when good luck prevails it is the proximity of bad that often bothers me and I can't enjoy myself but can only reflect on how close I am to the other. We climbed a remote mountain on the isle of Eigg once. Near the top, wearing only stupid sandals, Tracey slipped. I caught her just in time and pulled her up. She could have fallen a long way. We were so badly dressed. We sat in the low, swirling cloud, lonely, fortunate and foolish, wanting to be home, frightened by bad luck's proximity.

It doesn't do to dwell on my bad luck, nor does it do to bury it, but it takes time to understand it and to round it into the good times. I thought that as I was driving.

The sun was warm and the sky as clear and fresh as the morning glory that grew by the roadsides. Gulls wheeled overhead in the coastal towns. In Watch Hill, Rhode Island, where we stopped overnight, there was good surf and warm waves. The morning before we left, I slipped into a new pair of size small mustard-orange shorts with a drawstring waist – half price in an end-of-season sale – and waded into Long Island Sound. The sandy floor was gravelly and pebbled. I stuttered forward and then leant out, timidly pulling myself through the water in a half-hearted breast-stroke. My stomach muscles felt weak. The waves were welling up, swollen and strong. I bobbed above them. I could see Tracey on the shore, under the umbrella, watching me all the time.

When the big wave came I couldn't rise above it. It crashed down on my head, surging and bubbling. It dragged my body down. I let go for a moment. I felt free and unafraid. I gave myself up. And then I was staggering to my feet in the shallows, happy and victorious. And I could see Tracey on the beach, laughing and clapping her hands.